The basic book of

ROCK GARDENS
AND POOLS

The basic book of

ROCK GARDENS AND POOLS
W. E. Shewell-Cooper

Drake Publishers Inc. **New York**

Published in 1973 by
Drake Publishers Inc
381 Park Avenue South
New York, N.Y. 10016

© W. E. Shewell-Cooper, 1973

Library of Congress Cataloging in Publication Data

Shewell-Cooper, Wilfred Edward, 1900–
    The basic book of rock gardens and pools.

    1. Rock Gardens.   2. Water Gardens.   I. Title
SB459.S353   635.9'672   73-3372
ISBN 0-87749-483-5

Printed in the United States of America.

Contents

Illustrations

It may seem peculiar to some people to write a chapter on the reasons for rock gardening, but there are many who have an idea that the only possible reason for rock gardening is that a large number of rocks can be used. I can think of a dear relation of mine who made several rock gardens in her time, or rock gardens so-called, which seemed to consist merely of a fairly level bank on to which a large number of odd pieces of brick-bats, huge stones and broken marble slabs, etc., had been thrown. Between these unnatural looking 'rocks' various plants were put in and the whole thing as a result looked ugly and most artificial.

A rock garden should be made in order to accommodate the plants that like growing under particular conditions. After all, there are hundreds of plants available that have been collected from the Swiss Alps and from the mountains of India, China, Peru, or from other parts of the world. These plants, growing naturally at a high altitude, like particular surroundings. In their natural habitat they may be covered with snow throughout the winter and then in the summer the sun may beat down upon them. Where they grow they are probably much closer to 'King Sol' than in our own gardens at home.

These plants are used to having plenty of ice-cold water at their roots, and though they are covered with snow in winter the cold is dry and they can live happily throughout the frosty weather. As will be seen later on in the book they may have to be given a certain amount of protection in the winter for this very reason.

Another reason for rock gardening is that it is possible to grow very large numbers of dwarf plants. They are small and because of this, a great many of them can be put into a confined space. They are free flowering and have among their number some with the most glorious colours. Further, they can stand wind better than almost any other class of plants.

The rock garden, then, should be an attractive proposition for the small gardener as well as for those with quite a large area at their disposal.

A rock garden usually attracts womenfolk because it is comparatively easy to look after. It is slightly raised, or at any rate most parts of it are, so that the necessary hoeing and titivation can be done without continual bending. As many of the Alpines like barren soil, weeds do not grow so

A Waterfall in the Rock Garden

luxuriously, and so it may be necessary only to do a little hand weeding among the plants. It is useful for the man or woman who finds it difficult to obtain organic manure, for providing the pockets for the plants have been properly 'made up' they remain productive for many years without the addition of more humus-forming material. What top feeding is done can be in the form of special compost (as advised on page 31.

Providing good weathered rocks are used, the rugged appearance of this form of gardening is also a special attraction. The flatness of the lawn and the formality of the rose garden are a necessity, and so, if one wants some pleasant contrast and a sense of height, depth and distance, the careful placing of rocks in the rock garden will produce the right effect. It is wonderful the way the rock garden can make a garden seem larger.

Some people complain that the disadvantage of a rock garden is that it is in flower and looking beautiful in the spring and then is somewhat dull for the remaining months of the year. This book shows that it is possible to have a succession of flowers throughout the various seasons and so from early spring until late in the autumn this part of the garden can be an attractive feature.

It will be noticed that the term 'rock garden' has been used throughout this chapter in preference to that of 'rockery'. The rockery may be a mass of rocks while the rock garden can have fewer rocks, providing they are properly placed.

A rock garden need not be expensive though perhaps the original cost may seem to be high; for if this initial cost is rightly spread over a period of years, as well as compared with other forms of gardening, it will be found to be a comparatively cheap proposition. The fascination of this side of horticulture is surely due to the daintiness of the baby plants and to the wonderful variety that it is possible to obtain. Once the rock gardening fever sets in, an enthusiast is born, and this enthusiasm lasts for a lifetime.

The combination of the rock and water garden is natural since this so often happens in nature. The marrying of the two together is quite a simple matter. It is merely, so to speak, the leading of the one into the other. So often at garden shows you see a little stream wending its way down through the rocks, perhaps splashing over what looks a perfectly natural waterfall and then flowing on calmly and serenely over some shaley surface into a natural pool beyond.

The word 'natural' has been used on purpose, for to have a purely formal pool would be a travesty. Such a pool will have an uneven outline and may be semi pear-shaped or any shape at all to fit in with the surroundings but it must not be square, rectangular, oblong or perfectly round.

Naturally the choice of the site for the rock garden differs from garden to garden, but it must be borne in mind that it should be placed where the plants can be viewed to the greatest advantage. Equally, it must be where the plants will get the maximum amount of sun (at least for most of them). The reader will thus gain some idea as to the best place in which this particular garden should be made.

To make a rock garden in the shade of a tree is criminal, for the Alpines planted there will just wither and die. Not only is such a spot sunless, but the soil round about is robbed by the roots of the tree and so is poor. But probably the most serious danger to the plants is that caused by the drip, drip, drip of water from the branches, plus the falling of dead leaves in the autumn. It cannot be over-emphasized that many Alpines much dislike damp winters and the addition of drips from the branches of trees would certainly mean death. Collections of dead, soggy leaves around the plants always cause them to rot off, if not continually cleared away. This means a great deal of extra work.

As a rule the rock garden should not be near the house. There are exceptions, i.e. in cases where a rock garden slopes up to the south side of a house, say, built of local stone.

If there should happen to be any undulation in the garden and the particular spot concerned is sunny, this is ideal, for the rocks can be placed there and the necessary height and depth obtained without any artificiality. A low spot is sometimes chosen because it is the only suitable place, and if it is, then some form of perfect drainage should be carried out. This may mean filling in with large clinkers to a depth of 18 in. to 2 ft. In addition, a certain amount of agricultural pipe drainage may be necessary to carry the excess moisture away.

If there is to be a path right down the rock garden, then it should traverse naturally along the lowest part. Some excavation may be necessary in order to give the right effect, for if this is done the plants are more easily seen when they grow happily between the rocks on either side of the path concerned.

Where the garden is small and there is no definite depression, a mound with varying contours may be raised to the south side, with a path skirting its irregularly shaped outline.

Arrangement of rocks. Note no hard or straight edges and natural arrangement.

Preferably the site should be where the rock garden can be made a separate feature. A narrow bed of flowering shrubs may be used as a division – or the garden may be screened in some way, and though this is not an absolute necessity, it does in fact mark the division between the rock garden and the rest of the garden, thus enabling the gardener to fit it into the general scheme, apparently informally.

The rock garden should be as natural as possible. In a moderate-sized garden it would be a mistake to place it near the formal beds, or even in sight of them. These two features have nothing in common. In smaller gardens, where perhaps there is no room for a 'proper rock garden', the herbaceous or shrub borders may be edged with rocks, with Alpines planted in pockets between them.

It must be remembered that although an open aspect is desired, some plants revel in full sun, while others prefer a cool, partially shaded spot, and these various aspects may be obtained by careful placing of the rocks themselves.

It is very nice to have beautiful weather-worn limestone. Water and weather-worn limestone is also very attractive – but not everyone can afford to buy rocks brought from long distances.

It is often advisable to make the rock garden with stone found in the district. In the first place it will be cheaper, and secondly, it may look more natural. If this is done, it is better for the stone to be dug out of the hillside, almost intact, than for it to be quarried out of the bowels of the earth. Stone on the surface has been weathered, and so shows the markings of water and the original geological outlines. These help to give a natural appearance and, incidentally, make it easier to build up the garden in the way Nature would like.

Stone that is quarried cannot fail to have a newish appearance and is more difficult to lay in the soil in a natural formation. It has, however, been used on many occasions with great effect, because the designer had vision and could see what would look right and natural. The best side of the rock should always be visible and the unnatural-looking quarried edges should be hidden beneath the soil. All stones have to be set quite deeply and so this should be easy to do.

When buying stone, the fact that three-quarters of the

bulk of each one of them will never be seen, should always be borne in mind. It is so easy to look at the rock as a rock exposed and away from its natural surroundings and not to see it properly placed in position, with perhaps only a small portion of it in view.

Use rocks with a massive appearance, even if there are comparatively few of them, rather than use a larger number of smaller ones. For the bigger garden, there should always be two stones at least that weigh half a ton each, with the remainder weighing say, three cwt. each. For quite small rock gardens, the two main stones should weigh five cwt. and the others one cwt. each. It is difficult to be dictatorial but this is a plea for the use of 'rocks' rather than 'stones'.

Artificial Rocks I hate anything artificial – but there have been those who have found it too expensive to buy natural rocks who have made 'rocks' themselves with concrete. The method adopted is to dig a large irregular hole in the soil to the shape and size required. The bottom of the hole should be sprinkled with sand or any other material that will give the surface of the rock the colour and texture desired.

The following mixture of concrete is then used : one bucket of loose cement, four buckets of damp sand and five-eighths of a bucket of water. The sand and cement should be mixed together first, and the water should be added gradually. The amount of water mentioned should just be enough to give a really stiff concrete mix. This should be placed in the hole. Embed old jam pots, tins, etc., in the centre for lightness and economy, making sure that these are well covered with the concrete. The surface should be finished as required and sand sprinkled on top.

The 'rock' should be left to harden in its hole, which usually takes two or three days. It may then be dug out carefully and the surface can be altered somewhat – if it is really necessary – by scoring it with a trowel.

The main drawback to concrete rocks is that it takes some time for them to weather. The rapid growth of lichen will be encouraged if the surface of the rock, when dry, is painted with liquid cow manure or a mixture of flour, milk and water. In a few weeks, it will probably be difficult to distinguish home-made stones from natural stones.

It is not easy to make a large natural-looking rock at the first attempt, but some amateurs have done it with success.

They have been able to improve on my suggestions by putting irregular-shaped material in the bottom of the hole so as to give the appearance of stratification and weathering.

One man bought one or two good natural rocks and then used them to make earth moulds into which he could cast the cement. He could thus produce others of a similar size and shape. The disadvantage of this was that the rocks in the garden looked too similar.

To sum up this chapter : (1) The rocks should look as natural as possible; (2) They should be as large as possible and yet in proportion with the garden. It is often quite 'right' for them to be of the stone natural to the district; (3) A great deal depends upon the setting.

3 Building the Rock Garden

Few people want to construct a rock garden one year and then pull it down the next. When a rock garden is properly made it is made for good – or at least for a large number of years. It is, therefore, of great importance to give careful thought to the placing and the layout, even before the stone has been actually ordered or even before a spade has been put into the soil.

In the same way that the builder with his red bricks has to learn about English and Flemish bonds when arranging his 'courses' so the maker of the rock garden must learn about stratification and the laying of stones at the right slopes. The pockets where the plants are to grow must be provided in the places where nature provides them herself – on the back, at the sides and below the rock. Consider as well the area in between – where the rain may have deposited a layer of fine soil and semi-decayed organic matter over some rock which lies beneath.

The man who builds a rock garden must be able to see the end at the beginning, he must have a reason for its 'starting' and an equally good reason for its 'leaving off'. The picture must be complete. It is no good trying to thrust the rock garden of a big mountain into a small garden. The gardener must have the whole of the perspective in mind. Somehow his innermost being will tell him how big or how high, how wide or how long his rock garden should be.

You can get far better ideas for the home rock garden by studying small outcrops on hillsides, than by looking at some massive cliffs. It is from such natural outcropping that the meaning of the word 'stratum' may be understood as applied to the rock garden. Even then stratification should not be overdone and rigid lines emphasized in consequence. Strata in nature often consisted of bands of rock of the same thickness originally, but owing to the uneven durability of the stone or to some upheaval, the plainness of the line has been broken up and several bold blocks may easily appear within the strata.

Sometimes the density of the deposit varies. After all, the course of stratification is depositing by water thousands of years ago. Presumably, the material had time to dry year by year and so the matter was built up just as if piles of slates were laid one upon the other somewhat unevenly. Follow this, say, by an upheaval caused by an eruption or an earthquake, and the piles of slates can be split unevenly or be upended or torn asunder. Despite these happenings the lines of stratification always appear. There may be the primary line showing how and where the original material was deposited, and there may be secondary lines caused by the upheaval, whatever it may have been.

The depths of the layers would vary either because of the unevenness of the depositing matter or because of the subsequent wearing away by wind or water. In a similar way the depth of the stone used for the rock garden can vary from say one ft. to five ft. when building up the general lines of the stratum. It is possible to decide the thicknesses when considering the picture in hand. It is useful to start with the idea of forming a miniature hill and to use for this purpose the biggest piece of stone available, in order to convey the impression of height, rather than of actually building a high mound.

It is not necessary to start with a mound, for the lower stones when placed in position may give the necessary hint of greater height and so soil may be brought up to that point. On the other hand it is always necessary to start at the lowest part of the rock garden and to bed the lower rocks in their right strata well into the ground, i.e. at their right angle.

They should be put in sufficiently deeply to make them look like a natural outcrop and they must incline towards the main bed of soil in which they rest. The backward slope of the big rocks which are used, helps to get the rain down to the roots of the plants and not to take it away from them. Other rocks will then be placed in position and the 'tilt' will either be to the right or to the left.

The general slope of the strata should be followed when placing the other rocks, and so the small garden will be made with one general indicative slope but with the occasional glimpses of the upheavals that occur in nature. Thus vertical joints may be caused, some of them running parallel to each other and perhaps even parallel to the face of the rock.

The rock garden is to be regarded as the natural range of outcropping in miniature. Before placing the stones in position, look at them carefully and see if there are any particular markings. These may well determine where the stones are to be placed. Look at the graining and the weather markings and watch for the varying colours, and then try to blend these one into the other so that they become naturally part of the whole. Stones with really well-marked grainings are much easier to lay in position than rocks like the harder limestones or granite, in which the marks do not stand out. It is important not to move the rocks about too much on the soil or otherwise they would get stained or muddied up, and then it is not so easy to recognize the markings and to fit them into the picture.

The markings may not only be those of horizontal lines which show the strata, but there may also be the typical vertical marks produced by rain or frost or upheavals. These may well determine whether the stones are in their right position or not. Keep the same 'types' of stone together. Sometimes several rocks will be used together so as to build up a substantial 'block'. At other times it may be possible to use a really big stone to represent what may be called the solid core of the whole of the strata. Thus it will give the impression that this has survived the weathering effects of the wind, frost and rain, and may easily have round about it numerous smaller rocks representing the decay of the larger blocks of stone that were once its neighbours.

Having taken the utmost care, study the rocks to make certain they are being placed in their right position. A big group is often better than several smaller ones. Choose the more rounded stones for the top of the rock garden, for these give the right appearance of gradual weathering. The more angular stones look out of place here. The solid, harder stones will go in the lower part, especially by a stream or water side, for it is only if they were really hard that they would have persisted under these conditions. As the stones and rocks go into position, place suitable soil behind them and round about them, and ram this tightly so as to keep them in position. The so-called 'pockets' or planting areas will appear quite naturally. Sometimes these will be large, but even here it is possible to have small rocks peeping through.

Where rocks are to be placed above others, it is advisable to separate them by means of hard stones. These 'pit props' serve to prevent the soil between them from becoming squashed. The upper rock should always stand back from the lower one, and should not overlap or overhang. This is important. Do note, when looking at nature's rock gardens, how often the rocks are in pairs, one being smaller than the other – very much like a sheep and her lamb.

4 The Rock Wall and Crazy Paving

It is seldom that one finds an absolutely level garden and even when one does, it is advisable, from the point of view of a good design, to try and ensure at least two levels. This makes the garden so much more attractive. Great interest can always be assured by accentuating the difference between the levels in the making of a rock wall, which will later be well furnished with suitable plants. The bank between two terraces can also be made into a wall garden, the steps from the top to the bottom terrace even being clothed with plants growing in between the cracks.

The rock wall may be a retaining wall, built against the bank and the soil behind it will keep it moist and will provide an extensive cool root run for the plants. Sometimes special rock walls, frequently called 'dry walls', are built to serve as a division between two parts of the garden, taking the place, as it were, of the hedge. In this case, the soil dries out more quickly, and so plants which will tolerate dry conditions must be used for furnishing it. In both cases the soil must be free from weed roots, for when these are present the weeds will undoubtedly work their way through the rocks and so cause trouble in years to come.

Varying types of stone may be used for building such a wall, but the best are undoubtedly the fairly flat rough stones which are 3 in. to 8 in. thick. These should be laid one on top of the other, the spaces in between being packed firmly with a compost similar to that mentioned on page 31. Large enough cracks should be left to accommodate the roots of plants without cramping them too much. The stone should always be laid at a slight slope so that rain-water is allowed to drain down to the roots of the plants instead of dripping off the surface, and to prevent the stones at the top falling out of position.

Most people like to have a solid base to ensure that there is no chance of sinkage, and thus they lay the first two courses of rock work in cement and wait until this has set properly before completing construction of the wall. The face of the wall itself can slope slightly backwards, especially in the case of the retaining wall, because if it is built vertically, the weight of the soil behind tends to force it forwards. The angle need only be very slight.

It is always better to plant as the building of the wall proceeds. So decide upon the plants that are to be used before you start, and make certain that you have them on

Small plants covering cracks in risers

Rock-fringed garden steps

the spot ready when commencing construction of the wall. Providing that the roots are spread out properly, and good soil is used to fill in the spaces, no harm will come to the tender roots.

It is a good plan to try and arrange a successive display, starting for instance with the Aubrietias and yellow Allysum and continuing on with the Helianthemums, some of the Campanulas and ending up, say, with Sedum Sieboldii.

Furnishing an old wall   In some gardens, brick walls or old stone walls have already been built. These may well be made more attractive by filling in the larger cracks and crevices with a good compost (such as advised on page 31) and growing rock plants in these. It is sometimes possible to make cracks with a hammer and chisel. In addition, the tops of dwarf walls can be made into small strip beds by the judicious use of stones and bricks, a good soil mixture being placed in position to a depth of about 6 in. I have known quite good effects occur just by sowing seeds of some of the neater-growing annuals in cracks in the walls. The following annuals are quite suitable : candytuft, brachycome, cheiranthus, Dianthus heddewigii, escholtzia, felicia, bergeria, linaria, nemesia and ursinia.

Plants to use   The following is a list of plants which you can use in your rock wall. Make a choice of these. You will find full details of them in the list given in Chapter 11. Again may I remind you to make certain that the plants you choose cover as long a flowering period as possible, and either make up your mind to have a complete range of colours, i.e. red, pink, yellow, purple, blue, white, rose, orange and lilac, or else if you prefer, plan to have a wall of one colour only.

Name of Plant	Colours	Flowering
Aethionema vars.	Pink and white	April – August
Alyssum vars.	Yellow	April – July
Arabis vars.	White and pink	April – June
Armeria	White, pink and red	May – August
Aubrietia	Blues, mauves and reds	April – May
Campanula vars.	Blues and white	May – September
Cerastium	White	May – June
Cheiranthus vars.	Orange, yellow and lavender	April – July
Corydalis	Yellow	July – September
Dianthus vars.	Reds, pinks and white	June – August
Dryas	White	June – August

Erinus	Red, pink and mauve	June – August
Erodium vars.	Red, yellow and pink	June – September
Erysimum	Yellow and lilac	April – July
Gazania splendens	Orange	June – September
Geranium vars.	Reds, pinks and white	June – September
Gypsophila vars.	Pink and white	June – August
Helianthemum	Red, pink, yellow, flame, etc.	June – August
Hippocrepis	Yellow	June – August
Hypericum vars.	Yellows	July – September
Iberis	White and mauve	April – June
Linaria vars.	Mauve, pink and white	June – September
Lithospermum prostratum	Blue	May – September
Nepeta	Blue	June – August
Onosma vars.	Yellow and white	June – September
Phlox vars.	Pinks, mauve and white	May – June
Polygonum	Pink	August–September
Saxifraga vars.	Red, pink, yellow and white	April – August
Scutellaria	Violet	July – August
Sedum vars.	Yellow, pinks and white	June – August
Sempervivum	Yellow and reds	July
Silene vars.	Pinks and white	May – August
Thymus vars.	Pinks, mauves and white	June – August
Tunica	Pink	June – September
Veronica vars.	Blue and pink	June – August
Zauschneria	Orange flame	August–September

Laying crazy paving

Flagged paths and crazy paving are useful in other parts of the garden beside the rock garden. It does, however, seem particularly right to have a stone path leading to the rock garden from perhaps the lawn or through, say, a little wild garden. The charm of these paths (in addition to the pleasing nature of the stone used) lies in the fact that there are many dwarf rock plants which can be grown between the stones, and most of them do not object to a certain amount of treading on. They must not be laid just to resemble street paving. Too often a building contractor is given the job and he gets on with it, filling the joints in between with cement, and the effect is not natural.

The stones should be arranged so that they are level, with their flat surfaces upwards and with about an inch of space between them. The area for the path should be excavated and levelled evenly to a depth of at least 6 in. Very often at the 6-in. depth a thin layer of coarse clinker or ashes or even stones is laid, and on this a 1-in. layer of sifted ashes may be placed. The surface should consist of

the original soil which must be free from the roots of perennial weeds and be enriched with good horticultural peat
at the rate of half a bucketful to the sq. yard, plus some
fish fertilizer at the rate of four oz. to the sq. yard. Having
raked this soil mixture level, the paving may now be laid
in position.

It is a good plan to peg down tightly two lines running
the length of the path parallel one to the other. If the path
is to curve then pegs should be arranged close together,
so that the lines may continue to be equidistant even though
the path is to turn round a corner or 'wave' slightly. The
stones, when put down, should be made firm so that they
do not rock when walked upon. The straight edges of the
stones should be put along the line, so that the unevenness
appears towards the centre of the paths, the edges remaining quite straight. The stones should be arranged quite
level, and it is as well to have a builder's spirit-level available plus a fairly long plank, so that this may be assured.

Some people prefer normal crazy paving; others like
more formal types of paving (as set out in the drawings
on page 122). As a rule the crazy type of path is more
suited to the rock garden and the more formal type of paving to the surrounds of a square or rectangular pool. It is
easier to use crazy paving too if the path is to wander about
the garden.

As in the case of the rock wall, it is permissible to plant
in the cracks of the crazy paving as the work proceeds, but
there is a difficulty sometimes as a result of keeping the
levels right. Some people purposely chip off corners of
some of the stones so as to leave a space large enough to
put in a plant. If the plants go into position as the path
is being made, there is no difficulty at all in furnishing the
path in such a way as to make it look very attractive indeed.

**Furnishing
the path**

The types and kinds of plants used in crazy paving are
quite different from those used in the rock wall. The aim
should be to use plants which do not mind being trodden
underfoot. It is nice to have plants with scented foliage,
and there are a number that fill this bill. When they are
trodden on, aromatic perfume is wafted into the air. I refer
to the creeping mints and the prostrate growing thymes in
particular. There is at least one annual, Ionopsidium
acaule, which looks particularly attractive when growing

in between paving stones. It only grows half an inch high or so, and produces masses of pale mauve flowers. You only have to sprinkle the seed on the soil in the cracks early in April – very thinly – and it is not long before the plants are through.

Plants to use

There are plants of all kinds that can be used for growing in between crazy paving, some which only grow 1 in. high or less, and others which produce neat little tufts up to 6 in. in height. It is possible to arrange to have flowering plants of different colours – crimsons, pinks, blues, whites, purples, mauves and yellows, as well as plants with grey foliage, glaucous foliage, mottled foliage, marbled foliage, bronze foliage, scarlet and silver foliage, and, of course, fragrant foliage.

All the plants need very little attention. Some of the taller, growing ones will need an occasional thinning, or the removal of seeding heads, dead foliage or straggling stems. It is better to plant during the spring, when the Alpines will become established more quickly.

Mention has already been made of one annual that is particularly suitable for growing in between crazy paving, but the following plants may also be used if desired. The seeds are sown in late March and early April, where the plants are to grow, and when they have finished flowering they should be removed. Many of them conveniently seed themselves for the following year.

The plants I have used with success include Asperula setosa azurea (12 in. high with numerous, sweet-scented pale blue flowers); Clintonia pulchella (4 to 6 in. high with blue and white flowers); Leptosiphon hybridus (3 in. high with flowers of various colours); Virginian stock (6 to 9 in. high, various colours); Sanvitalia procumbens (6 in. high with single or double yellow flowers); and Myosotis dissitiflora (9 in. high with large early flowers).

Suitable Alpines for Crazy Paving

Name of Plant	Brief Description	Flowering Period
Achillea vars.	Glaucous or bronze leaves, red fruits	June – July
Aschillea vars.	White or yellow	May – September
Ajuga	Blue	May and June
Antennaria vars.	Pink and white	June

Name of Plant	Description	Flowering Time
Arabis	White	April – June
Arenaria vars.	White and mauve	May – July
Armeria vars.	Pinks and white	May – August
Aubrietia vars.	Mauve to deepest red	April – May
Bellium	White	Summer
Campanula vars.	Blues and white	May – September
Cerastium	White	May – June
Cortusa	Bronzy green leaves	April – May
Dianthus vars.	Reds, pinks and white	June – August
Dryas	White	June – August
Erinus	Mauve and red	June – August
Frankenia	Pink	Summer
Globularia	Blue	June
Gypsophila vars.	White and pink	June – August
Helichrysum	White and yellow	June – August
Hieracium	Orange red	July
Hypsella	White and crimson	June – July
Linaria vars.	Purple and pink	June – August
Lysimachia	Yellow	June – September
Mentha	Mauve	June – September
Oxalis vars.	White and yellow	Summer
Phlox vars.	Pinks, lilacs and white	May – July
Raoulia vars.	Silver and green leaves	
Polygonum	Pink	August-September
Sedum vars.	White, yellow and pink	June – August
Silene vars.	Pink and white	May – August
Thymus vars.	Pink, red and purple	June – August
Veronica vars.	Blue and pink	May – August

Now we must consider the question of soils for the rock garden. Naturally the ordinary person in the ordinary garden will make use of the soil that is already there, doing all that can be done to make it as suitable as possible for the usual run of hardy rock plants, and only making up special beds or 'pockets' for those plants that are unlikely to thrive in the main section.

Time and again the phrase 'a well-drained soil' is used. What exactly is meant by that? It is by no means the same thing as a dry soil, but it does mean that the soil will not become dank and waterlogged during winter. This well-drained condition is assisted where the rock garden is elevated above the general level of the garden, but that alone is not always enough – the result is often nothing more than poor, dry soil.

The soil itself can be improved by the addition of various ingredients. Of these the most important is plant 'fibre' of some sort. Get a load of sods that have been cut, grass and all, from an established pasture. These sods will be about 5 in. thick and should be piled, grass side down, in a good square stack for about six months, by which time all the vegetation should be well rotted. Chop this 'fibrous loam' into small pieces, about the size of a hen's egg, and mix it well with the garden soil. The presence of the fibre in the new loam will help to keep the soil open and well-drained, without being poor.

If it is impossible to get hold of fibrous loam, use coarsish sedge peat instead, which is easily available. The addition of coarse sand is also a good thing, but do not add too much, as there are no plant foods in this. Only those plants for which a specially sandy soil is recommended would benefit by the addition of more than one part of sand to eight parts of soil.

Details of the soil mixture for plants appreciating scree conditions are dealt with on page 35.

Some plants require a 'lime-free' soil. Therefore in places where the natural soil is limey, it will be necessary to make up complete beds with lime-free loam and peat in equal quantities with one part in four of sand. Other plants such as Gentiana Farreri will thrive in a mixture of pure peat and sand. In all cases where a lime-free soil is needed, be sure that any covering in the form of stone chippings is also not limey. Any artificial watering should be done with rain water as far as possible, because places with a lime soil frequently have a water supply that also contains lime.

Planting the new garden

It is often convenient to plant a few of the larger features, such as the slow-growing conifers, at the same time as placing the rocks. These little trees are so much part of the framework of the design that their inclusion early in the proceedings helps one to picture the finished structure. Also, it is possible to get the roots well down into the soil if done early. Later on, the job of digging a large hole for planting a shrub is naturally difficult to do neatly.

Except for the large plants mentioned, it is best to delay normal planting until the soil has had time to settle. If the rock garden is constructed in autumn, delay planting until March or April.

Consider the placing of each variety. Be sure you have some idea of the appearance of the full-grown plant before you put it in; then you will be able to put it in a position where it will be seen to best advantage. People are generally aware of the dangers of colours clashing if badly arranged, but one can have terrible 'misfits' in size and habit of growth as well.

For positions where there is only a small pocket of soil it is always best to plant a young seedling. In this way it would be possible to get the plant well established. A large specimen would probably die of drought before it could root well down in the narrow cracks of rock.

When to plant As a general rule, it is best to plant up the rock garden in spring, even though that is very near the flowering time of some of the plants. Many small plants that grow quite happily if planted in March, would not have survived if moved in November.

Another time planting can be done satisfactorily is during the late summer, when many of the more rampant plants are being cut back and divided. This gives time for the newly divided plants to get well-rooted in warm soil, and form neat hummocks before winter sets in.

Most nurserymen grow their Alpine plants in pots, and, provided the plants are well rooted and healthy, it is safe to plant them at any time, even in full flower. If however the weather is very dry it is best to give the hole a good 'puddling' before turning the plant out of its pot and dropping it into the hole, and an occasional watering later will help it to get firmly established.

Plants for the beginner

Plant failure in the rock garden is a dismal sight, so the wise beginner will concentrate his energies on the obliging plants that are easy to grow. He will thus be encouraged by his early success and then rapidly leave the beginner's class and become a real enthusiast. There is a stupid kind of snobbery one meets – very seldom in real gardeners – that makes people want to look down on the plant that co-operates with the grower and will give a wholehearted display of colour, while they praise the sulky little plant that seems to grudge living at all, let alone giving more than an occasional bloom. Let us have none of that attitude. The garden that needs ruthless cutting back to avoid over-crowding is infinitely gayer in every way than the one that demands coaxing attention at all times.

The following plants will give a good display in the rock garden without your having to prepare any special soils. Just the ordinary garden soil, treated as recommended earlier in this chapter, and as much sunlight as possible.

Name of Plant	Colours	Flowering
Achillea	White and yellow	May – September
Alyssum	Yellow	April – July
Anthemis	White	July – August
Arabis	White	April – June
Armeria vars.	Red, pink and white	May – August
Aster vars.	Pink, mauve and blue	August – September
Aubrietia	Blues, mauve, pink and red	April – May
Campanula vars.	Blue, purple and white	May – September
Cerastium	White	May – June
Corydalis	Yellow	July – September
Dianthus vars.	Reds, pinks and white	June – August
Erodium vars.	Red, yellow and pink	June – September
Geranium vars.	Reds, pink and white	June – September
Geum	Orange, yellow and pink	April – September
Gypsophila	Pink	June – August
Helianthemum	Red, pink, yellow, white, flame, etc.	June – August
Hypericum vars.	Yellow	July – September
Iberis	White	April – June
Nepeta	Blue	June – August
Omphalodes	Blue	February – May
Phlox subulata	Pinks, mauve and white	May – June
Polygonum	Pink	August – September
Primula Juliae vars.	Pink, purple and mauve	February – April
Pulmonaria	Pink and blue	March – April

Saponaria	Pink	June – August
Saxifraga vars.	Red, pink, yellow and white	February – August
Sedum vars.	Yellow, pink and white	June – August
Silene Schafta	Rosy magenta	June – August
Thymus vars.	Pink, mauve and white	June – August
Veronica vars.	Blue and pink	June – August

There has been a certain amount of argument as to the difference between a scree and a moraine. Most books seem to treat the two as one, and use these two names alternatively. It is safer to regard the scree as a mass of rock debris and stones together with a certain amount of soil and sand brought down by a glacier and left behind when this receded. There are immense deposits of such material in the mountainous parts of Europe.

The moraine consists of similar material, but three feet or so below, a water pipe is laid and suitably punctured, so that a continuous underground stream of water is provided at will. It is seldom possible to do this today in view of the expense and lack of materials. Anyway it has not been found really necessary in this country, for it is very seldom, if ever, that the soil at that depth becomes dried up.

We can reasonably regard these two names as almost synonymous, but to satisfy certain readers, I am purposely including a few special notes on the moraine towards the end of this chapter (page 39).

It is only necessary to make a scree if you want to grow certain choice Alpines which will not thrive in ordinary rock garden soil. Many of the choicest plants *must* have perfect drainage, and only flower at their best when they are growing in very little soil indeed. Please do not make a scree and then grow in it the common plants that are perfectly happy under other conditions. Scree gardens are quite easy to construct and cheap to maintain and they may be made either on a slight slope or on the flat. A slope should never be too steep or the moisture may drain away too rapidly. If the scree is made on the flat, the bed should always be raised a little above the general level of the ground, say, 4 or 5 in. above.

As to the materials to be used in a scree, these should consist of a collection of small broken pieces of rock and plenty of chippings. Any kind of stone can be used – granite, mill stone grit, sand stone or even flint. All that is necessary is to dig out about 2 ft. of soil and put into the hole thus excavated big stones and rough material of any kind to provide drainage. Use smaller stones gradually towards the top with the finest ones on the surface.

With the granite chippings or mill stone grit, a certain amount of sedge peat, fine leaf mould, and loamy soil may be used. Gardeners differ as regards the proportion, but a mixture consisting of 15 parts of fine stone to 1 of soil and sedge peat mixed together would seem to be fairly common – and suitable. It is with the smaller stones which form the surface of the scree that this compost is mixed.

Select a sunny, slightly sloping site between, say, two bold rocks, so that the effect appears quite natural. The scree will then slope very, very gradually towards, perhaps, a stream or maybe a further stratum of rock below. Usually, however, it would be towards the base of the rock garden, and would be fitted into the plan as the work of construction went on.

Saturate the whole bed thoroughly while it is being constructed, and couple this with a good treading. Before the plants are put into position, shake all the soil from their roots, so that these may be spread out shallowly in the fine scree material. After planting follow with a good watering, so as to help the plants to settle down.

Some people like to have the scree in the higher parts of the rock garden, so that the plants, when they are growing, will be flowering at the normal eye level. It is then possible to enjoy the effect at any time. There are plants which are lime lovers and which prefer a surface of limestone chippings in the scree and others which hate lime and so need granite and sandstone chippings. You can provide more than one scree and so produce the right material for the various groups of plants to be grown. Naturally, in small rock gardens this is not possible, and the best idea under these circumstances is to have areas in the scree with limestone, while the bulk of the scree will consist of non-calcareous materials.

The great advantage of a scree garden is that very few weeds will grow there. The common garden weeds, such as groundsel and chickweed, prefer a good rich soil and cannot flourish in the poor fare provided by the stone chippings. When a scree has to be quite small, it is usual to give it a little variation of surface in order to prevent it looking monotonous and flat. The watering given after the scree has been made tends to wash away the bulk of the soil at the surface and so leaves a nice layer of pure material on the top. It is quite a good plan to have an occasional large stone in the scree so as to produce a natural effect and in addition to provide stepping stones for getting about among the plants.

**Furnishing the
scree**

Always plant the scree with young plants and preferably quite tiny ones. It is far more important to buy a plant with a really good root system and a small top than to buy what so many beginners seem to look for, and that is a plant with tremendous top growth and poor roots below. Plant the scree naturally. There will be no question of putting plants in straight lines. There may be a little group here, a stray plant there, a drift of glistening silver leaf plant towards, say, the edge, and so on. The planting must look natural and not spasmodic. Most scree lovers will want to include a widely representative collection. But don't over-plant, and remember that the Alpines are going to spread – so give them room to develop. Bear in mind colour harmony and try not to have such arrangements as puce pink next to bright crimson.

Plants to use

In order to help readers decide which plants to use in the scree, the list below gives brief descriptions and times of flowering. Further details of these plants will be found in Chapter 11.

Name of Plant	Description	Flowering Time
Acantholimon		
glumaceum	Light rose	June – July
Aethionema, all	Deep rose, pink	
	and white	April – August
Alyssum wulfenianum	Pale yellow	May – July
Androsace, all	Pink and white	April – October
*Anemone vernalis	Silvery white	March
Antirrhinum Asarina	Yellow	May – September
Arenaria purpurascens	Lilac	June
,, tetraquetra	White	May
Armeria caespitosa		
Bevan's Variety	Pink	April
Asperula, all	Pink and White	May – September
*Calceolaria biflora	Yellow	July – August
,, tenella	Yellow	May – September
Campanula allionii	Blue	June – July
,, arvatica	Deep violet	May – June
,, bellardii vars.	White and blues	June – July
,, cochlearifolia		
Cambridge Blue	Light blue	June
,, pilosa Superba	Pale blue	June – July
,, pulla	Purple	June – July
,, raineri	Blue	June – July
Convolvulus	Lavender	June – July
*stansfieldii		
mauretanicus	Blue	July – September

Name of Plant	Description	Flowering Time
*Cyananthus, all	Deep blue	July – August
Dianthus alpinus	Deep rose	June – July
,, arenarius	Pink	June – August
,, arvenensis	Pink	June
Dianthus myrtinervius	Pink	June – July
,, neglectus	Pink and buff	June – July
Douglasia vitaliana		
praetutiana	Golden	May – July
Draba aizoides	Golden	March – April
,, bryoides imbricata	Golden	
,, pyrenaica	Lilac	March – June
Edrainthus serpyllifolia		
major	Purple	May – June
,, tenuifolius	Pale lavender	June
Erigeron fletti	White	June – August
Erinus alpinus Dr.		
Hanaele	Glowing carmine	May – August
Erodium corsicum	Pink	June – September
*Erythraea diffusa		
centaurium	Pink	June
Euryops acraeus	Yellow	May – June
*Gentiana verna	Blue	May – June
Geranium argenteum	Rose pink	June
,, napuligerum	Pink	June – July
Globularia cordifolia	Mid-blue	June – August
Helichrysum milfordiae	Russet-pink	May – June
,, selago	Silver green leaves	July
,, virgineum	Pink buds opening to creamy white	July
Hypericum empetrifolium prostratium	Yellow	June – September
Hypsella longifolia	Purplish pink	June – September
Iris lacustris	Mauve and gold	April – May
Lewisia, all	Various	May – July
Linaria alpina	Purple and pink	May – July
Morisia monantha	Yellow	April – May
Onosma, all	White and yellow	June – September
Origanum hybridum	Pinkish hop-like	July – September
*Oxalis enneaphylla		
minutifolia	White and pink	May – June
,, inops	Deep pink	June – September
Papaver alpinum	Various	May – September
Pentstemon roezlii Hort.	Ruby red	May – June
*Phlox adsurgens	Shell pink	May
,, douglasii Boothman's Variety	Mauve with lilac centre	May – June
Polygala, all	Various	May – August
Polygonatum hookeri	Rosy lilac	May
Potentilla nitida	Pink	June – July
Primula auricula Dusty Miller	Yellow or red	May
,, marginata	Lavender	April
Ptilotrichum spinosum roseum	Pink	June – July
Rananculus montanus Molten Gold	Yellow	June – August

Raoulia, all	White, silver foliage	July
Saxifraga Encrusted (all)	White, pink and yellow	May – July
„ kabschia (all)	Various	February – June
„ oppositifolia latina	Clear pink	March
Scutellaria indica japonica	Dark violet	July
Sedum spathulifolium Oappa blanca	Yellow	July
Sempervivum, all	Red, pink and yellow	July
*Shortia uniflora	Pink	April – May
Silene acaulis saxatilis	Pink	June – August
*Soldanella, all	Violet	March – April
Statice bellidifolia (syn. Limonium)	Mauve	July – September
Thymus serpyllum coccineus	Red	July – August
Verbena chamaedryfolia	Scarlet	June – September
Veronica telephiifolia	Pale blue	July – August
Viola rupestris rosea	A pink-violet	July – September

Plants marked with a * can only do well in a lime-free scree.

The moraine

As stated earlier, there is no real difference between the moraine and scree, except that it is usually accepted that in a moraine water runs continually below the surface during the short period in spring and summer when growth is active. In nature this occurs because snow is continually melting at that time and the water thus trickles down underneath the scree material. In the winter, of course, the ground is frozen and covered with snow many weeks, and thus the plants are kept 'dry'. They hate damp winters.

Alpines that will not survive normal American winters because of dampness will thrive in a scree or moraine. This is particularly true of the woolly-leaved species. A moraine should face south and have a slope of, say, 1 in 16. It is made as a rule just above a path. The underground irrigation of the moraine is the nearest approach that anyone has been able to achieve to the conditions found in, say, Switzerland.

7 Shrubs, Conifers and Ferns

Shrubs are very useful in the rock garden, not only because they provide a background for the alpine plants, but also because they give shade when this is necessary, and protection. Furthermore, they are particularly effective in the winter time when so many of the normal alpine plants are not in bloom. Shrubs also improve the general look of the rock garden, but they must not be allowed to become too overpowering.

Whether flowering or evergreen, shrubs should be used with discretion. Where they prove most suitable, the number to be included will depend largely upon the size of the rock garden. Most of the shrubs recommended in the list at the end of this chapter are of a very dwarf character, others can easily be kept within bounds by the judicious use of a pair of secateurs. Never plant a shrub that has to be kept clipped regularly, as this looks far too formal. Some shrubs grow prostrate and so will screen a boulder, others are pointed and look like little pinnacles; some are evergreen, others lose their leaves in the winter; some have a round look, like little hedgehogs, and these are particularly slow-growing and diminutive in character.

It is always as well to choose some shrubs for their berries, or for their autumn and winter colouring, and some for the intrinsic beauty of their flowers in the spring and summer. Some, like the Acer dissetum, have the most lovely, finely-cut foliage which always reminds me of the plumage of some exotic bird. This group, by the way, love to have plenty of peat worked into the soil for them.

The baby rhododendrons also like plenty of peat and a soil which is free from lime. In the case of the smaller shrubs, don't put in a single specimen. Try to get a real splash of colour, especially in the case of a large rock garden. With the spire-like conifers – say, one of the Junipers – it is often possible to have one little sentinel alone, or perhaps one with a shorter friend beside him!

The deciduous shrubs (those that lose their leaves in the autumn), are best planted in the late autumn. The evergreen kinds are usually planted in April, although in the south some people go in for September planting. Ordinary soil will suit most of them. Where special soil treatment is needed, details will be found under the heading 'Remarks' in the list given on pages 43-44.

List of conifers suitable for the rockery

The list below gives the names of the most suitable conifers. Whilst some are dwarf by habit, others are only useful for the first 10-12 years or so of their life. Then they become too big to be good inhabitants of the rockery, and should be dug out. (Such plants are marked '°'.)

ABIES balsamea hudsonia. Has bluish-grey leaves, and is like a dwarf fir. Its ultimate height and spread respectively are 1½ ft. and 2 ft. It prefers a moist shady spot.

CEDRUS brevifolia. Very slow growing, and of stunted habit. The young leaves are bright green. The maximum height is 2 ft. and the spread 2½ ft. Its appearance is irregular but it is very beautiful.

CHAMAECYPARIS lawsoniana ellwoodii. Lovely blue-grey foliage and a good plant for the rockery. It is oval and dense in appearance.

° *C. l. Ellwood's Gold.* A golden foliage type of Elwoodii. When planted the height is 2 ft., but its ultimate height and spread are 8 ft. and 3 ft. respectively. It has a bushy and upright habit.

C. l. Ellwood's Pygmy. Has a distinctive appearance. It is wider than high, broadly rounded with age. Ordinary well-drained soil is best.

C. l. nidiformis. A low-growing conifer with bluey-green ostrich-feather-like leaves.

C. obtusa nana gracilis. A beautiful dwarf conifer with bright green leaves arranged in close whorls. It has a low, spreading and pyramidal shape.

° *C. pisifera filifera aurea.* The foliage goes golden yellow. Its height when bought is 1½ ft. but eventually it is 5 ft. tall and spreads 3 ft. The appearance is slender, but the branches are cord-like.

C. aurea nana aureovariegata. Very dwarf, slow-growing variety whose branchlets are tipped with gold. Is low and cushion-like in habit.

C.p. plumosa compressa. A pretty variety with broken golden sprays. Height 5 in. spread 12 in. Is low, flat-topped and spreading in habit. Very slow growing.

JUNIPERUS communis compressa. A dense cone-shaped bush, the foliage a glaucus grey, often called the 'Noah's Ark Juniper'. Plant 5 in. high. Will grow to 2 ft.

J. c. prostrata. Very low growing with grey-green foliage. While its height is only 4-6 in., the spread is indefinite.

The habit is prostrate and creeping.

J.c. repanda. A prostrate dense form. Branches less flat than 'Compressa'.

° *J. sabina tamariscifolia.* Low-growing and of spreading habit. The maximum height is 3 ft. and the spread is 5-7 ft. Is prostrate in flat tiers in appearance.

PICEA abies nidiformis. Very spreading. The tips of the branches a pale green in the spring.

P. glauca conica. A perfectly cone-shaped variety with bright green foliage densely packed. Height is 4½-6 ft. and the spread is 2-3 ft. Ordinary soil, well drained but on the moist side.

P. excelsa remontii. Very slow-growing variety. The leaves are a soft yellowish-green. Height is 2½ ft. and the spread is 2 ft. It looks broadly conical.

P. mariana Nana. Low growing, globose and dense. Foliage bluey-green.

THUYA lobbii occidentalis Rheingold. A beautiful variety with gold foliage in the summer, turning to bronzy-red in the winter. When planted may be 12 in. tall but is eventually 3-5 ft. It is globose or broadly pyramidal.

T. occidentalis globosa. A globular ball of bright green foliage. A fairly strong grower. Its height is 4 ft.

T.o. globosa (Little Gem). A miniature of the above with finer foliage. Height 2 ft.

T. orientalis aurea nana. Dense, globular and dwarf. Foliage light green.

A List of Shrubs Suitable for the Rockery

Name of plant	Description	Height	Season Flowering time	Remarks
Andromeda polifolia compacta	Grey leaves, pink, urn-like flowers, twiggy shrub.	1'–2'	April–August	Peaty soil, semi-shade
Anthyllis hermanniae	Attractive, bearing yellow broom-like flowers.	9"–1'	July–August	Most soils
Azalea hinodegiri	Bright crimson flowers. Evergreen.	2'–3'	April–May	Sandy, peaty soil, semi-shade
Berberis buxifolia nana	Orange yellow flowers, purple fruit. Dwarf compact evergreen.	2'	April–May	Most soils, sunny spot
B. thunbergii atropurpurea nana	Leaves purple. Vivid in autumn. Orange flowers and red berries.	12"–15"	April–May	Most soils, sunny spot
B. darwinii	Dark green leaves, orange yellow flowers. Evergreen.	6'–12'	April	Most soils, sunny spot
Cassiope tetragona	Tiny, bell-like flowers, pink, hanging from shoots on thread-like stems.	6"–12"	March–June	Moist, sandy, peat
Cistus crispus	Deep rose flowers 2 in. across. Evergreen.	2'	June	Dry, sandy, limey soil, full sun
C. purpureus	Purple flowers, marked in dark red.	3'–4'	June	See above
C. coeris	Low spreading, crinkled foliage, white yellow-centred flowers, crimson buds.	1½'–2'	June–July	Most soils
C. pulverulentus 'Sunset'	Large rosy carmine flowers.	1½'–2'	June–September	Very beautiful
C. pulverulentus 'Silver Pink'	Clear pink.	12"–18"	June–August	Almost any soil
Cotoneaster adpressus	Much-branched, prostrate. White flowers, red berries.	6"–9"	Autumn berries.	A nice shrub from China
C. congestus	Pinkish flowers, red fruit, Brilliant autumn foliage. Evergreen.	6'	April–May	Moist soil, chalky
C. horizontalis	Semi-evergreen. Pink flowers, red fruit.	3'	April–May	Moist soil, chalky
C. microphyllus thymifolius	Arching branches with pinkish flowers, red berries.	4'	April–May	Moist soil, chalky
Cytisus beanii (Broom)	Golden yellow flowers.	9"–12"	April–May	Light, well-drained, sun or partial shade
Cytisus kewensis	Cream flowers.	6"–12"	May–June	Light, well-drained, sun or partial shade
C. praecox 'Warminster'	Light yellow flowers.	3'–4'	April–May	Light, well-drained, sun or partial shade
Daphne blagayana	Creamy white, scented flowers, evergreen, spreading habit.	9"–12"	March–April	Well-drained, slightly acid soil or stony soil
D. cneorum	Fragrant, pink flowers. Evergreen, Trailing habit.	10"–12"	April–May	See above
Erica carnea vars.	White, pink or crimson flowers.	6"–9"	December–May	Sandy, peaty soil, sun or semi-shade. Lime tolerant.

Name	Description	Height	Flowering	Soil / Conditions
E. cinerea vars.	White, pink or crimson flowers.	6"–9"	July–September	Dislikes lime
E. mediterranea vars.	Scented, pink flowers.	4"–10"	March–May	Dislikes lime
Escallonia rubra pygmaea	Dwarf rock shrub, red flowers.	12"–18"	July–August	Very pretty
Euonymus fortunei 'variegatus'	Silver variegated foliage, flowers inconspicuous.	1'–2'	July–September	Semi-shade or under trees
Fuchsia procumbens	Brown and yellow flowers, large pink berries.	3"–4"	June–October	Sheltered sunny spot
F. magellenica 'Pumila'	Red and purple flowers.	12"–18"	June–October	See above
F. riccartonii	Red and purple flowers.	4'–5'	June–October	See above
F. Tom Thumb	Red and purple flowers.	8"–12"	June–July	See above
Gaultheria procumbens	Pinkish white flowers and bright red berries.	6"–9"	July–August	Peaty, limeless soil, some shade
Genista dalmatica	Rare species, like a dwarf gorse bush, gold flowers.	¾'–2'	June–July	Light, well-drained soil, sunny
G. hispanica	Bright green leaves and bright yellow flowers.		June–July	See above
G. pulchella	Very small growing, beautiful yellow flowers.	1'–1½'	May–June	See above
G. lydia	Prostrate habit, butter yellow flowers, allow to hang.	2'–3'	May–June	Any good soil
G. sagittalis (syn. Chamaespartium sagitale)	Golden flowers.	12"–18"	May–September	Light, well-drained soil, sunny
G. tinctoria flore pleno	Double golden flowers.	6"–12"	July–August	See above
Hedera helix minima	Yellowish green foliage.	1'–2'	Foliage all year.	Light, well-drained soil, sunny
Philadelphus 'Manteau d'Hermine'	Double white fragrant flowers.	6'–8'	June–July	Most soils, any position
Potentilla fruticosa vars.	Yellow, white and orange flowers.	1'–1½'	May–August	Any soil
Rhododendron ferrugineum (Alpenrose)	Many tubular rose pink flowers.	2'–3'	April–June	Deep, sandy soil, sunny spot
R. racemosum	White and rose pink flowers.	1'–2'	April–May	Will grow in limey soil
Salix wehrhahnii	Dwarf willow with silver catkins.	2'–3'	April–May	Dislikes lime in soil
Spiraea bullata	Scarlet rose flowers.	1½'–2'	July–August	A Swiss type
S. Anthony Waterer	Crimson flowers.	2'–3'	June–October	Moist loam, some shade
Syringa palibiniana	Compact, scented, lilac flowers.	1'–2'	April–June	Moist loam, some shade
*Veronica armstrongii	Golden leaves and white flowers.	9"	Summer	Perfume can be overpowering
V. cupressoides	Similar to conifer in appearance, white flowers tinted with lavender.	½'–3'	June–July	Any ordinary soil
V. hectori (Whipcord Veronica)	Lilac flowers.	1'–2'	June–July	
V. kulii	White flowers, crimson stamens.	2'–3'	June–August	
V. pinquifolia pagei	Glaucous blue leaves, white flowers.	6"–9"	May–June	
V. pimeleoides	Glaucous, blue grey leaves, purple.	½'–1'	June–July	
V. p. Polly Moore	Evergreen, Violet blue flowers.	1'	July–August	Sturdy, new

* Veronicas are now called Hebes!

Ordinary daffodils and tulips look out of place in the rock garden, being tall and 'gross' in comparison with their neighbours. There are, however, a number of baby bulbous and tuberous rooted plants which should be grown, since they add interest as well as colour to this garden. Many of them come from mountainous districts of Europe and Asia – the Pyrenees, for example, seems to specialize in the 'babies' of the narcissus species. As they have what may be called an Alpine background and birthright, they certainly deserve a place in our rock garden.

Planting should be done in late summer or early autumn. The autumn and winter flowering plants must be in by August, but September or October is quite soon enough for planting those which bloom in the spring. The taller-growing kinds such as the Alliums, Anemones, Fritillarias, Sternbergias and Tulip species should be planted from 3 to 6 in. deep, depending on the size of the bulb (the smaller the shallower) and 4 to 8 in. apart (the dwarfer the closer they go). The remainder of the bulbs in the list which follows may be planted from 1½ to 4 in. deep, and from 1 in. to 3 in. apart, according to the size of the bulb.

Most of the plants enjoy an open situation with all the sun they can get, and will thrive in ordinary soil. Exceptions are the Colchicums and Sternbergias which require a fairly deep, rich soil; the Anemones which seem to like a rich and moist soil; and the Trilliums which prefer partial shade and a moist, peaty soil.

When once established, the majority can be left down for a number of years. Little attention is needed beyond keeping down weeds and clearing away the withered foliage at the end of the growing season. The Tulips, perhaps, will benefit by being lifted and rested each year, or at least every two years, and also the Irises, in all but the warmest districts.

List of bulbs for the rock garden

ALLIUM. Miniature onion-like plants with narrow leaves and heads of small flowers.

> *A. albopilosum.* Large heads of lilac flowers, one of the finest for planting in groups. Very suitable for cutting. 2 ft. June.
>
> *A. azureum.* A handsome tall-growing kind bearing globular heads of deep sky blue flowers. 2 ft. June-July.

A. giganteum. Substantial umbels, distinct rose tinted violet, a real giant. 4 ft. July.

A. karataviense. This is a most distinct Allium with very broad flat leaves; the scapes are about 8 in. high and bear dense umbels of pink to rose coloured flowers in May.

A. ostrowskianum. Exquisite and distinct variety for the rockery with carmine pink flowers. Grows to about 6 in., producing a mass of bloom. June.

A. rosenbachianum. Large heads of purple lilac flowers on 3½ ft. stems. Very handsome planted in the neighbourhood of rhododendrons. May-June.

A. sphaerocephalum (descendens). Handsome heads of crimson maroon, beautiful cut flower for floral work. 2 ft. July.

ANEMONE. The brightly coloured large-flowered kinds are well known. Those species suitable for the rock garden are similar but daintier and altogether smaller.

A. blanda. Blue flowers. There is also a pink variety. 6 in. January-March. Requires rather a sheltered position.

A. fulgens. Vivid scarlet flowers with a black centre. There is also a double variety. 12 in. May. Requires a partially shaded position.

A. nemerosa allenii. Lavender-purple flowers in January-March. 6 in.

A. ranunculoides. Clear golden-yellow flowers. 6-12 in. March.

BRODIAEA GRANDIFLORA. Bright blue clusters of flowers in June. 6 in.

BULBOCODIUM VERNUM (Meadow Saffron). Violet flowers in January. 4-6 in. Very free-flowering.

CHIONODOXA. Dwarf plants with small hyacinth-like leaves and 2 or 3 flowers per stem.

C. luciliae. Bright blue flowers with white centres. There is also a white and pink variety. 4-6 in. March.

C. sardensis. Gentian blue flowers with a white centre. 4-6 in. March.

COLCHICUM. Plants with crocus-like flowers but wider leaves, similar to those of a daffodil.

C. agrippinum. Small lilac purple blossoms checkered white.

C. autumnale major (byzantinum). Purplish-pink flowers.

6-8 in. September-October.

C. autumnale roseum plenum. A beautiful double rosy mauve.

C. speciosum illyricum. Rosy-purple flowers. September.

CONVALLARIA MAJALIS. (Lily of the Valley). White scented flowers in May. 1 ft.

CROCUS. The smaller-flowered species are more suitable for the rock garden than the larger-flowered, garden varieties.

C. imperati. Inner petals violet, outer petals fawn. 6 in., January-March. The earliest crocus to flower.

C. medius. Attractive little oval flowers of lavender purple with brilliant flame-coloured stigmata.

C. ochroleucus. Long milk white heads on slender stems, vivid orange stigmata and orange base within. A most dainty-looking species.

C. pulchellus. Lavender with paler veins and a golden throat. 6 in. Autumn.

C. salzmanni. One of the loveliest autumn flowering crocus; the outer segments are oblong gradually tapering to a short point and of a beautiful lavender blue colour; grassy leaves produced at flowering time which is an additional attraction.

C. sativus. Purplish-lilac, feather with violet. The stigma is long and blood red in colour. 6 in. Autumn.

C. speciosus. Violet-blue flowers, veined with deeper violet and orange-red stigma.

C.s. aitchisoni. This variety is light blue.

C.s. Conqueror. Most effective large rounded flowers of soft violet blue, gold flush at base, bright orange gold stigmata. One of the showiest autumn crocus.

C. tomasinianus. Pale blue flowers. 3 in. March.

C. versicolor. White flowers, faintly striped with purple and a yellow throat. 6 in. March.

C. zonatus. Rosy-lilac. 6 in. Autumn.

C. chrysanthus seedlings. Various colours.

CYCLAMEN. Dwarf species are all hardy. Autumn flowering kinds should be planted between January and July. Spring flowering kinds from July to September.

C. coum. Deep rosy-red. 4 in. February-March.

C.c. album. Dainty blush white petals, deep red purple eye.

C.c. crimson. Deep rose.

C.c. roseum. Oblong petals of a lovely light pink shade.

C. ibericum. Similar to C. coum but the leaves are marked with silver. 3-4 in. February-March.

C. neapolitanum. Rose-pink flowers and ivy-like leaves marked with silver. 4 in. Autumn. The flowers are out before the leaves appear.

C. repandum. Bright crimson flowers with silver marbled foliage. 4 in. March and May.

ERANTHIS. This cheery little plant is well known. The flowers are bright yellow, similar to, and about the same size as, those of a buttercup. There is a green frill just below each flower.

E. cilicica. Slightly larger flowers. 3 in. Spring.

E. hyemalis. Long-stalked leaves. 3 in. January-March.

ERYTHRONIUM. These are small plants with flowers shaped something like those of a cyclamen.

E. americanum. Yellow flowers, spotted red. 6 in. April-May.

E. denscanis. Rose-pink flowers. 3-6 in. April-May.

E.d. Lilac Wonder. Long broad tapering petals of lovely columbine pink combine with prominent blue black anthers to make a most graceful and distinguished flower.

E.d. Purple King. The broad tapering petals of heather purple reflex gracefully from the blue black anthers and the gold centre dappled with chocolate brown, giving a tiger Lily effect to these elegantly poised flowers. Rich green leaves heavily marbled with chocolate brown.

E. grandiflorum. Yellow flowers. 6-9 in., April-May.

E. revoltum White Beauty. A species of serene loveliness, claiming a place with the elite of alpine plants. Often two flowers on one stem resembling miniature lilies with swept back petals of purest white bearing a profusion of cream anthers which hang down within a rugged circle of indian red with a soft yellow flush at the throat, attractive marbled leaves. April-May.

E. tuolumnense. A fine variety of vigorous growth producing two to three handsome flowers of buttercup yellow on long slender stems; fine glossy unmottled foliage. This orchid-like species is invaluable as a cut flower for small vases; extremely beautiful rock plant.

FRITILLARIA. These plants have drooping bell-shaped

flowers, beautifully marked with fine lines.

F. *citrina*. Pale yellow flowers. 8-12 in. May.

F. *meleagris*. Purple and cream-coloured flowers. 12 in. April and May.

GALANTHUS. These bulbs are extremely useful because they are so early flowering.

G. *byzantinus*. The large white flowers are marked with green. 8 in. January.

G. *elwesii*. The large white flowers are marked with green. 8 in. January.

G. *nivalis flore pleno*. An exquisite double form of the common Snowdrop.

Snowdrop, Galan-thus nivalis

G.n. *maximus*. Very large flowering variety, vigorous habit.

IRIS. The best known kinds suitable for the rock garden are some of the dwarf bulbous sorts. On the whole, they are early flowering.

I. *alata*. The flowers vary from lavender-blue to deep lavender, with a golden keel. 6-12 in. January.

I. *danfordiae*. Yellow and brown flowers. 3 in. February.

I. *histroides major*. Blue, yellow and violet. 6 in. February.

I.h. *Reine Immaculée*. A delightful species, in all respects identical to *histroides major* except for its colour.

Silky flax blue standards and falls the same colour deepening to hyacinth blue at the mouth, white tongue with golden yellow line and inky blue flecks.

I. reticulata. Sweetly-scented, deep violet-purple flowers with yellow markings. 6-12 in. February.

I.r. Cantab. A plant which is equal to the type as regards beauty and hardiness. The dainty flowers are a misty cobalt blue with deep Cambridge blue falls and tongues of orange.

I.r. Clairette. This is indeed a lovely little iris. Its erect crisp standards are a clear violet blue which shows off the really vivid gentian blueness of the velvety falls with their narrow ivory tongues marked with the same gentian blue.

I.r. Springtime. Soft pale blue standards, falls deep violet purple with narrow purple lines and spots merging into the ivory white tongue, the pointed petals are prettily reflexed.

I. tuberosa (syn. *Hermodactylus tuberosus*). Velvety black falls, standards greenish without rich colouring. Curiously sombre but quaint, worthy of a place in the rockery amongst the brighter subjects. Popular for floral arrangements. March-April.

IXIA. These are taller than the majority of the plants, but they are attractive and graceful, several flowers being produced on a wiry stem. There are many varieties, varying in colour from white with red or dark purple centres to yellow, orange, pink or red. Some are double. 12-21 in. May-July.

LEUCOJUM AUTUMNALE. White and pink flowers. 4 in. October.

L. vernum. (Spring Snowflake). These charming little white bells tipped with pale green look delightfully fresh during February-March. Strong bulbs, flowering first season.

MUSCARI. (Starch or Grape Hyacinths). Small plants with bluebell-like leaves and heads of small flowers tightly packed together, not unlike a bunch of grapes.

M. botryoides. Pure white flowers. There is also a dark blue variety. 6 in. March.

M. moschatum. Greyish-purple flowers. 6 in. March.

M. paradoxum. Bluish-black flowers. The darkest of all. 6-7 in. March and April.

M. plumosum. The spike of violet flowers has a feathery appearance. 6 in. April.

M.p. Heavenly Blue. A beautiful sky blue.

NARCISSUS. There are a number of 'baby' daffodils, all quite hardy.

> *N. bulbocodium.* The leaves are narrow and the rich yellow flowers have a cone-shaped trumpet. 6 in. April. Prefers a moist situation. There are also pale yellow and white varieties.

> *N.b. conspicuus.* (The Hoop Petticoat). Bright yellow.

> *N. cyclamineus.* Rich yellow flowers; the petals are reflexed, making the flowers similar in appearance to a cyclamen flower. The leaves are narrow and rush-like. 6 in. February and March. Prefers a moist situation.

> *N. minimus.* The smallest of all trumpet daffodils. Flowers are citron-yellow. 3 in. February.

> *N. minor.* Another small trumpet daffodil, golden-yellow in colour. 6 in. March.

> *N. moschatus.* White with pale citron-coloured cup. 12 in. April.

> *N. triandrus albus.* A small creamy-white narcissus with reflexed petals.

> *N.t. calathinus.* Similar to above with larger flowers. 6-7 in. March.

ORNITHOGALUM ARABICUM. Fragrant, star-like white flowers with black centres. 18 in. June.

> *O. nutans.* Silvery grey and pale green. March.

> *O. umbellatum* (Star of Bethlehem). White. May.

PUSCHKINIA (Striped Squill). The flowers, of which a dozen or more are borne on a spike in a similar manner to Hyacinths, are very pale silver blue with deep Prussian blue lines down the centre of the petals. A sunny and well-drained position suits them best. April.

> *P. libanotica (schilloides).* A pretty type.

SCILLA. Dwarf plants with bluebell-like leaves and bell-shaped flowers, one or two per stem. Enjoys partial shade.

> *S. bifolia.* Deep blue flowers. 3-6 in. March.

> *S. sibriica.* Bright blue flowers. 3-6 in. February.

SPARAXIS. These are most wonderful plants for rock work where their richly coloured flowers produce a gorgeous effect. They delight in a light sunny position and should be well covered during the winter. 6 in. May-June. Mixed varieties only.

Narcissus triandus albus

STERNBERGIA COLCHICIFLORA. Yellow flowers. 4 in. September.

> *S. lutea major.* Effective crocus-like flowers of a rich golden yellow colour. 12 in. September.

TULIPA. Several of the tulip species are suitable for the rock garden. They are smaller-flowered and more graceful than the ordinary garden varieties.

> *T. batalinii.* The fine pale yellow flowers of this lovely species show up extremely well against the creeping ribon-like leaves. 4 in. May.

> *T. chrysantha.* This lovely little Himalayan Tulip is ideal for the rockery. The three outer petals are pure rose carmine merging to buff at the base; the insides are pure buttercup yellow with no variation in tone. Foliage is narrow, long and upright. 6 in. April.

> *T. eichleri.* Extremely effective and beautifully sculptured Tulip of shining scarlet; the petals look as though they have been polished, and reflex slightly. Coal black centre with a narrow band of yellow. 12 in., April.

> *T. greigii.* The flowers are a glowing vermilion-scarlet tinted with orange. The leaves are spotted. 9-13 in. May.

> *T. kaufmanniana.* The petals are creamy-white with a golden base inside, and a dull, strawberry-red broad stripe outside. There are many beautiful named varieties.

> *T.k. Berlioz.* Produces a very lovely neat flower with a charm all its own. Clear daffodil yellow opening to citrus gold, petals are slightly pointed at the tips, foliage distinctly mottled purple brown. 5 in. April.

> *T.k. Gaiety.* Vivid soft cherry panel on the outside of the petals with an ivory border, interior of ivory with a golden yellow centre, very dwarf, the flower gives the impression of a water lily. 4 in. March-April.

> *T.k. Robert Stolz.* This very dwarf Tulip only grows 4-5 in. high but the flowers are such a brilliant scarlet that they show up well in spite of their small size. They are self-coloured except for a centre of yellow and black. The leaves are broad and distinctly marked with dull purple. April.

> *T. pulchella.* Rosy-mauve flowers. 6 in. May.

Propagation

Rock plants may be propagated in four ways : by seeds, division, cuttings and layers. Anyone keen on a rock garden is advised to take some interest in the raising of new plants, for the life of the average Alpine is about 5 years. A brick frame, facing north, is an ideal place for raising young rock plants. A well-built brick or concrete frame keeps cool and, facing north, does not dry out so quickly. The young plants can be placed here, in their pots, plunged up to their rims in ashes. The lights need only to be put into position if the weather is very wet, and even then, wooden blocks can be put underneath, so as to lift them up to allow free ventilation. During frosty weather, the lights may be closed if the plants have been watered recently.

Seeds

Raising plants from seeds does ensure that they will be healthy and vigorous. It is a good method of acclimatizing imported strains, and of raising new varieties. The seeds should be gathered just as they become ripe and are ready to fall (they should never be gathered green). They should then be placed in a shallow receptacle and baked in the sun for a week or so, before being put into packets or being sold. When packeting, be sure to label immediately.

The main batch of seeds should be sown during February and March. Then plants will be quite strong enough to be put out in the early autumn. Plants that are raised from midsummer sowings will be planted out the following spring.

Many of the ordinary varieties may be sown in a seed bed with a western aspect. It should be sheltered. The soil should be dug to a depth of 8 in. and made friable. It should be quite clean and free from weeds. If the soil is inclined to be sandy, horticultural peat sedge may be worked in, at 4 or 5 oz. to the sq. yard. Sow the seed thinly, in shallow rows 6 in. apart, and then cover with a thin layer of sterilized soil.

If you know that the seeds are slow germinators, it is quite a good plan to sow mustard in the rows. This marks them, and allows hoeing to be carried out. Should the weather be dry, watering through a fine rose may be necessary, and if slugs are a nuisance, put down metaldehyde bait. Where only a few seeds are to be sown, or where the variety is rare, it is worth while sowing in pans or pots.

These should be crocked to about a third of their depth,

the crocks covered with sphagnum moss and the pans filled up with a non-soil compost. The seed should be mixed with three times the quantity of sand, and then sown thinly. A little of the compost should then be sifted over the top from a fine-meshed sieve.

A sheet of glass should be put over each pan, and this should be removed each day and wiped dry to remove the condensation. Watering should be done by plunging the pans up to the rim in a bucket of tepid water for a minute or so. Plunge the pots up to the rim in coconut fibre or moss when they are growing, as this will preserve the moisture also. When the seeds have germinated, the sheet of glass may be removed, though it is a good plan to water the plants by immersion as before.

Stand out during a snowy winter, and allow the snow to lie on the pans. Extremes of temperature often help germination. Seeds sometimes take two years to germinate, and in this case it may be advisable to sprinkle sand over the pan from time to time to reduce the growth of moss.

The compost may be altered somewhat to suit the likes and dislikes of various plants. For instance, more peat can be added for the Ericas and Rhododendrons, more sandstone for the Androsaces and a little more limestone for the Saxifrages.

Division

When the plants are propagated by a vegetative method, they are true to type and come quickly to maturity. Division should be undertaken immediately after flowering, the roots being broken up into small pieces with roots attached. If pots are used, these should be placed in a closed frame for two or three days, and plunged in ashes until the roots are properly established. When potting, place some sand round the roots so as to ensure drainage and to prevent them from damping off.

Some plants, like the Androsace, send out runners like strawberries, and these can be made to grow in little pots sunk into the ground round about the plant, or in the compost. In the case of Primulas and Auriculas, the crowns are divided quite easily. With various Dianthus and Phlox, many of the stems will be found to be rooted, having come into contact with soil. These rooted pieces can be severed and potted up. In the case of Sempervivums and some Saxifrages, the rosettes die after flowering, leaving a ring of young rosettes behind. These usually take two or three years to form a flowering rosette in their turn.

Cuttings

Soft wood cuttings. New young shoots are used for this type of cutting, the best time for taking them being just after flowering. If the old flowering shoots are cut back, young shoots are encouraged to grow, and may be taken off when anything from $\frac{1}{2}$ to 2 or 3 in. long. The stem should be cut through square with a sharp knife, just below a leaf, or a pair of leaves. The lower leaves should be removed but it is a mistake to remove any above the soil surface.

The cuttings may either be rooted in pots or in a frame. The latter should have 2 to 4 in. of damp sand on top of the soil. The cuttings are just pushed into this and watered in. They must be potted up as soon as they are rooted, since there is no food in the sand.

The pots should be well crocked to provide plenty of drainage, and filled with a compost consisting of one part loam, one part leaf mould and one part sand, all passed through a $\frac{1}{4}$-in. sieve before mixing. The cuttings should be put firmly round the edge of the pots and watered in. These pots are then placed in a closed frame, which should be aired for about half an hour each day and shaded from bright sunlight. The pots should not be watered more than is necessary.

Each cutting should be potted up singly when the roots are about $\frac{1}{2}$ in. long, and the pots kept in a closed frame for a day or two, before plunging them into ashes in an open frame.

Hard wood cuttings. These are of vigorous, well-ripened shoots taken in late summer. The lower leaves should be removed and the cuttings rooted in pots, cold frames, or in a sheltered position outside.

Layering

Some plants which do not come true from seed, are also difficult to propagate from cuttings, but will often root when layered, e.g. Ericas, Rhododendrons, Daphne.

A branch near the ground should be chosen, and cut nearly through with a long, slanting cut. The cut is kept open by means of a small stone or piece of stick, and the branch is pegged down firmly into a heap of sandy compost. The end of the branch should be tied to a bamboo, to prevent it from being blown out of the ground before it has rooted. If a branch is too high up to reach the ground, the best plan is to break a pot longitudinally in half and tie it, full of compost, round the cut branch, or to use a sleeve of polythene tied at the ends. Watering will need to be done frequently in hot weather.

Layering is usually done in autumn, and the branches are examined the following spring. If they have rooted, the branch is severed between the parent plant and the newly-formed roots, and the layer may be moved a month or two later. It is important to keep the soil moist from the time of layering until the new plant is well rooted.

All pot Alpines are best kept plunged in ashes or fine gravel. In this way the soil is kept from drying out, the temperature remains fairly even, and the pots are not so liable to crack in frosty weather.

Routine Cultivation

The routine cultivation of the rock garden may be divided into three definite periods, (a) Spring, (b) Summer, (c) Autumn.

Spring The whole of the garden may be given a light top dressing with a compost consisting of one part good soil (sterilized if possible), one part silver sand, and one-quarter part horticultural peat or rotted leaves. The whole should be rubbed through a $\frac{1}{4}$-in. sieve. It is necessary to work some of this compost in among the tops of the mossy Saxifrages, but this can only be done on a dry day and when the plants are in a dry condition. The compost must be really dry also. The rosettes may be packed tightly in this material. If there is any moisture about they will rot off.

Any rocks that have been loosened by frost during the winter should be made firm. Soil in the pockets that has been loosened should be packed down firmly, and any soil that has obviously been washed away should be replaced. See if any of the plants on the steeper slopes have been washed away, and replace them. Should the weather be dry, copious watering will be necessary. In an attempt to hold in the moisture, place small pieces of stone around the choicer plants.

Everything should be done to keep down weeds and so prevent seeding. This means a fair amount of hand-weeding, an operation which is not as tedious in the rock garden as it is in the flat formal bed. A three-pronged carving fork will be found useful for disturbing the weeds and for breaking up the ground. A hoe should never be used in a rock garden, for it destroys the Alpine seedlings which are so often worth keeping.

A look-out should be kept for slugs and other pests at this time, and a determined effort to control them early in the year will save a lot of disappointment later.

Summer   Keep on weeding and hand forking all through the summer, though if the weeding has been thorough in the spring, there is not much of this work later. The surface of the soil should be stirred with the hand fork from time to time. If the summer is hot it may be necessary to give thorough waterings occasionally, and after each soaking the soil should be loosened again, so as to keep a surface mulch. As each plant ceases to flower, the flowering heads should be removed, unless they are being left on for seed-saving purposes. The straggly plants should certainly be cut back after flowering, and it is often necessary to cut them back quite hard. Certain of the older plants may need dividing, cuttings may be taken from some plants, and seeds saved from others.

Autumn   This is the time for a certain amount of renovation. Some old pockets of hardier plants will need disturbing, because the soil is exhausted, and they can then be cleared out, re-made, and re-planted. The dead growth should be cut back, and any leaves from trees that fall on to the rock garden should be removed immediately. The woolly-leaved plants should be protected by sheets of glass; this prevents them from damping off from excessive moisture. Plants that need particular attention in this connection are Raoulia, Androsace and Asperula.

A sheet of glass should be erected 5 or 6 in. above the plant and parallel to the surface of the soil. This is all the protection the plants require. It is not advisable to cover them with a tent cloche. It can be supported on a simple wire bracket.

Pests and diseases in the rock garden

Plants in the rock garden do not suffer from the attacks of pests and diseases to the same extent as do vegetables and fruits. Cleanliness in the garden is the best preventative. Where the removal of fallen leaves and other loose rubbish is carried out thoroughly, the insect population is reduced, because it is under such rubbish that many insects lie hidden all the winter.

SLUGS AND SNAILS. These can be very troublesome in spring, eating off the tender young shoots as they start to grow.

Control. The best scheme is to poison them. Bait can be bought ready to use. The bait should be spread on the rock garden where the slugs are known to be.

WOODLICE. These are a nuisance, nibbling through stems at ground level and feeding on young roots.

Control. Derris powder sprinkled about the ground near large stones or by cracks where the woodlice congregate will soon remove these pests.

WIREWORM. These are sometimes introduced in new loam. Examine the loam carefully when preparing it. and remove any insects. Trapping with pieces of carrot stuck in the ground, should remove those missed at first. (Carrot attracts wireworm.) Examine the pieces each morning, and remove and kill any insects found in them.

APHIS. The usual collection of Greenfly, Blackfly and other 'colours' of this all too well-known pest will attack rock plants at all stages.

Control. The secret of successful control is to start early – a day's delay after the first fly is seen allows time for literally hundreds more to be hatched out. Spray with insecticides containing nicotine or derris, and give additional sprayings at intervals afterwards to kill off any 'stragglers'. Alternatively, a dust containing the same substances can be used. This would be better for plants that do not like damp.

EELWORM. This minute pest is invisible to the naked eye, but its effect will be recognized in the rock garden, where it often attacks Cheiranthus. The new growths look very 'bunchy', like the Robins-pin-cushions seen on wild roses.

Control. The only practical control in the ordinary small garden is to pull up and burn all infected plants, and only take cuttings from those that show no sign of the complaint.

MILDEW is the only disease likely to cause damage in the rock garden, and that only in dull, damp weather.

Control. Prevention is the best cure in this case. A healthy plant, growing in a suitable position will seldom suffer, and attention to good drainage is the first step in the battle against mildew. Dusting with Flowers of Sulphur will help to prevent the spread of the disease, if an attack does start.

10 A - Z of Rock Plants

ACAENA. New Zealand Burr. Low-growing carpeting plants inconspicuous flowers and attractive foliage in various shades. Very suitable for paving and steps as they stand up to a certain amount of traffic. They grow in practically any soil and manage to thrive in sun or shade. Do not plant them near any of the weak growing treasures because they quickly cover a large area. Increased by division.

> *A. adscendens.* A study in silver-purple and brown foliage. Summer. 3 in.

> *A. buchanani.* Pale silvery green leaves. Inconspicuous flowers in July and August. 2 in.

> *A. glaucophylla.* Blue foliage, red stems and red burrs. 4-6 in.

> *A.g. 'Greencourt Hybrid'.* Glaucous leaves turning to bronze and covered with red burrs. Summer. 3 in.

> *A. microphylla.* Tiny bronze foliage and large spiny, globular crimson burrs; slow growing, most attractive. Summer. $\frac{1}{2}$ in.

> *A.m. inermis.* Bronze leaves slightly larger than the preceding. The dull little flower heads are borne on 4-in. stems.

> *A. novea-zelandlae.* Deep green, oak-like leaves, red burrs. Good ground coverer. Summer. 4-6 in.

ACANTHOLIMON. Prickly Thrift. The plants form a mound of spiney leaves just like a grey green hedgehog, covered in June with sprays of flowers. They need a position in full sun and require a very well-drained soil. Propagation is difficult and only a small proportion of the cuttings taken will form roots, but these should be taken in summer and put in a sand frame.

> *A. glumaceum.* Flowers light rose in June, 6 in.

ACHILLEA. Milfoil. Many of these are common wayside herbs, and all have aromatic foliage. Useful for the mat of grey or green leaves which make good winter carpet, as well as producing a mass of flowers in early summer. Will grow in any light, well-drained soil in full sun. Increase by division, which can be done successfully directly after flowering when the dead heads are being removed. This gives the plants time to form neat tufts before winter sets in.

> *A. ageratifolia.* Silver tufts, pure white head. May-July. 6 in.

A. *argentea.* Silvery leaf. Clusters of white daisy flowers in June, 6 in.

A. *chrysocoma.* Greyish woolly foliage, yellow heads. May-June. 6 in.

A.x. kellereri. Finely-cut greyish foliage and white heads. June-October. 6 in.

A. *lewisii.* (Syn. King Edward). Grey-green leaves. Flowers a delicate sulphur yellow. These appear in succession from May till September. 9 in. Definitely the most useful owing to its long flowering season, and colour which blends so well with other flowers. Not so rampant as the others, and needs to be lifted fairly frequently and the young pieces replanted in good soil, otherwise it tends to exhaust itself by over-blooming, leaving the young shoots very weak.

A. *rupestris.* Smooth green leaves. Heads of white flowers in June, 6 in.

A. *tomentosa.* Green ferny leaves. Flowers bright mustard yellow in July. 9 in.

AETHIONEMA. The ones grown in rock gardens are mostly miniature bushlets and deserve a place in every collection. They need full sun and do best in a light, well-drained loam which contains some lime. Can be easily raised from seed which gives healthiest plants, though the named hybrids have to be increased by cuttings of the young shoots which appear after flowering. Keep the plants cut back after flowering and they will remain neat bushes for many years.

A. *armenum.* Warley Rose. Neat little wiry bushlet with grey green leaves. Long spikes of rose pink flowers in May. 9 in.

A. *coridifollum.* Small bushes, pale mauve heads. May-July. 6 in.

A. *grandiflorum.* Similar to the above, but generally longer lived and will reach 18 in. high when well established.

A. *iberideum.* Prostrate growth. The greyish leaves are nearly circular. Small clusters of white flowers in May. 4 in.

A. *oppositifolium.* Silver tufts with pink heads. Choice plant for scree or alpine house. June-July. 1 in.

AGATHEA. A shrubby blue daisy from South Africa. Needs a light sandy soil and a position in full sun. Though not really hardy, it is so easily raised from cuttings that it is well worth growing. Produces a good show of flowers throughout the summer and on into the autumn months. A few cuttings put into a pot of very sandy soil and kept in a frame during the winter will provide replacements after a hard winter.

> *A. coelestis.* Clear true blue with golden centre. One-year-old plants are about 9 in. high, but those that have managed to survive several winters will attain 18 in. or more.

AJUGA. Bugle. Gout Ivy. With no claim to great beauty they are invaluable carpeters, growing in any soil and even managing to flower in damp, shady sites. Spread very quickly by means of runners and should not be planted too near less vigorous plants or they will choke them.

> *A. pyramidalis.* Pyramidal spikes of gentian-blue with ultramarine. May-July. 6-8 in.
>
> *A. reptans purpurea.* Leaves of a reddish purple. Spikes of blue flowers in May and June. 6 in.
>
> *A. reptans variegata.* Like the above, but the leaves are variegated with pink and cream.

ALLIUM. The 'Mountain Garlic'. Grow in well-drained soil in sun or part shade. Bulbs should be planted fairly deeply. All types are attractive.

> *A. cernuum.* Deep lilac-rose heads. June-July. 12 in.
>
> *A. farreri.* Reddish-purple. June-July. 9-12 in.
>
> *A. macrostemon.* Purplish-pink. Dainty heads. June-July. 6-9 in.
>
> *A. mairei.* Small grassy tufts, heads of pale pink. 4 in.
>
> *A. narcissiflorum.* Beautiful. Bears nodding umbels of bell-shaped rose coloured flowers. July. 4-6 in.
>
> *A. senescens glaucum.* Attractive. Curry bluish foliage and pink heads. June. 6 in.

ALYSSUM. Madwort. Gold Dust. A large family of hardy annuals and perennials, only a few of which are worth a place in the rock garden, but those few include some of our showiest spring flowers. They like a light well-drained soil, not too rich and preferably containing lime. The more sun they have the better. Plenty of space is advisable as a well established patch of old plants is a magnificent sight and gives a greater display of bloom than the same area planted up with young plants. Increased by seed, except the double flowered variety.

A. montanum. Semi-prostrate species with green leaves and mustard yellow flowers in summer. 6 in. Rather too rampant for the amount of flower, but useful in a rock wall.

A. saxatile. Strong yellow flowers in April to May. 9 in. The well-known Gold Dust used for bedding.

A.s. compactum. A neater-growing form of the above and more suitable for rock gardens.

A.s. citrinum. A lemon yellow form. When raising from seed, it is advisable to flower the young plants to make sure they have come true to colour, specially if they are intended for a position where the strong yellow of the ordinary form would not look well.

A.s. Dudley Neville. A pale buff hybrid.

A.s. flore pleno. A double-flowered form which holds its flowers longer than the singles. Cuttings are best taken with a heel just after the plant has flowered.

A. spinosum roseum syn. *Ptilotrichum.* An uncommon little shrublet. The flowers are a washy pink and of no particular value, but after they fall the stems that remain harden into spines which give the plant a silvery white appearance all through the winter. 12 in.

A. wulfenianum. Silvery foliage, prostrate. Large pale yellow groups of flowers.

ANACYCLUS. The 'Mount Atlas Daisy'.

A. depressus. Ferny-like greyish foliage, white, scarlet-backed daisies. They close in the evening and then the scarlet reverse looks beautiful. Easy to grow in sun. May-June. 2-3 in.

ANDROMEDA. 'Bog Rosemary'. One of the 'heather' family. Makes a nice compact specimen.

A. polifolia 'Compacta'. A tiny Rosemary, with pink flowers. No lime please. Partial shade. April-May. 6-9 in.

ANDROSACE. Rock Jasmine. True Alpine plants that need care during damp winter weather, which makes them rot off at ground level. They must be planted in very well-drained soil, and most of them like lime and need a position in full sun. The majority of them have greyish-green leaves covered with silver hairs. These hairs are for protection from the dry cold of intense frosts in their native habitat, but are a drawback in our climate as they hold the winter moisture which is the plant's worst enemy. A sheet of glass arranged over the plants during winter will help them to survive, and a layer of coarse limestone chippings around them assists good drainage. The plants may be divided, but better results are obtained from cuttings. Single rosettes of the current season's growth are put in a sand frame and root easily. When it is required to get a large patch quickly, the rooted cuttings may be planted out two or three together, and each rosette should give a flower head the following season.

A. lactaea. Stiff shiny leaves. White starry flowers on branching stems in June. Sets seed freely which make nice little plants in a year. 3 in.

A. lanuginosa. A trailing species with lovely silver leaves. It is at its best planted above a large rock where it can fall down in a mass. Flower heads of mauvish pink are produced throughout the summer on 6 in. stems, but as these too are prostrate, the whole plant does not reach that height.

A.l. leitchlinii. As the above, with white flowers that have a distinct red eye.

A. mucronaefolia. Similar to *sempervivoides,* only much tighter in growth. Pink umbels. Summer. 2-3 in.

Rock Jasmine, Androsace sarmentosa

A. sarmentosa. One of the best for the rock garden, being hardier than the usual varieties. Spreads quickly and has produced some fine named hybrids. Umbels of pink flowers from May to July. 6 in.

A.s. var. *watkinsii.* Deep pink.

A.s. var. *Yunnanense.* Strong pink, and rather larger than most varieties.

A. sempervivoides. Rosettes free from hairs, so the plant is better able to resist damp. Flowers bright pink in April. 3 in.

ANEMONE. Wind Flower. Only a few of this family are suitable for the rock garden, most being woodland plants. They generally look best if planted in combination with a low carpeter such as Thymus serpyllum. Soil should be good and fairly deep, and the position open but not too scorched in summer. Those varieties that are raised from seed will do best if the seed is sown as soon as it is collected, at which time it will germinate well. Keep a regular watch for the ripening seeds as they seem quite firmly fixed one day, and a couple of days later have all blown away.

A. magellanica. Charming South American plants which bear deep cream flowers followed by cottony seed heads. May. 6-9 in.

A. vernalis. See *Pulsatilla vernalis.*

ANTENNARIA. Cat's Ear. Close carpeters which are very useful for paving or as ground cover through which taller plants may push their way. Will thrive in ordinary soil, provided it is not too wet. Easily increased by division.

A. dioica rubra. Neat dark green foliage. Flowers deep pink in June on 6 in. stems.

A.d. tomentosa. Leaves more attractive, being silvery, but the little white flowers are very dull.

ANTHEMIS. Camomile. This herb needs a poor, light soil or it becomes too rank. Given a place in full sun, it makes a good background for spring bulbs planted between the clumps. Increased by division.

A. biebersteinii. 'Rudolphiana'. Feathery silver foliage; golden-yellow flowers. Sun, any soil. June-August. 6 in.

ANTHYLLIS. A prostrate little plant, not unlike a clover, to which it is allied. In ordinary light soil in a sunny position it will spread into a large plant. Increased from cuttings of soft side shoots in summer.

A. hermanniae. Attractive, tiny, shrub bearing lots of yellow broom-like flowers. Summer. 9-12 in.

A. montana rubra. A mat of grey-green leaves. Flowers crimson in June. 3 in.

AQUILEGIA. Columbine. Some of these well-known

plants are very suitable for the rock garden, especially the lower growing species. The commoner types should be avoided as they seed too freely and tend to become a nuisance. Ordinary soil, and positions in sun or semi-shade. Easily grown from seed, but home-saved seed is often a failure as the different varieties cross very easily and it is the commoner types that predominate in the resultant hybrids.

A. *alpina*. Clear blue flowers. Suitable for naturalizing where there is plenty of space. 18 in.

A. *flabellata nana*. Nodding flowers of cream and violet. 3 in.

A. *flabellata nana* '*Alba*'. Lovely pure white form. 6-9 in.

A. *glandulosa*. Beautiful clear blue flowers with central petals white. 12 in.

A. *longissima*. An attractive species with yellow flowers that have very long spurs in May. 18 in.

A.*l*. *Crimson Star*. A beautiful crimson flowered variety.

A. *pyrenaica*. A dwarfer form of A. *alpina*.

ARABIS. Rock Cress. A large family of which a few are invaluable in the rock garden, while many others are worthless little weeds. Very useful in walls as it thrives in hot, dry situations. Poor soil with plenty of lime suits it best. Increased by division or cuttings, some species are best raised from seed.

A. *caucasica*. Low mats of green leaves which spread very quickly. Valuable because of the earliness of its white flowers. 9 in.

A.*c*. *flore pleno*. Like the above in habit, but the double white flowers are a great improvement, and hold longer, though coming into bloom a little later. April to June. 9 in.

A.*c*. *variegata*. Leaves liberally marked with yellow. Flowers single white.

A.*c*. '*Pike's Crimson*'. A lovely colour. Flowers spring and summer. 3 in.

A.*x*. *suendemannii*. Rich rosy-pink flowers. All Summer. 4 in.

A. *sturri*. Rosettes of shiny little leaves. White flowers. 4 in.

ARENARIA. Sandwort. The members of this family vary in their requirements and are best treated separately.

A. *balearica*. A close carpet of little green leaves that will clothe the bare rock face, if planted in a moist position in semi-shade. Covered with tiny white flowers in May and June, which accounts for its popular name of 'Spilt Milk'. 1 in.

A. montana. Forms a loose mat of wiry stems that scramble over rocks and through small shrubs. Huge white flowers in June and July. 6 in. Needs light soil and a sunny position. Easily raised from seed.

A. purpurascens. Shiny green leaves, lilac starry flowers in June. 2 in. Not showy enough to be grown alone, but makes a good carpet for the weaker growing early bulbs.

Sandwort, Arenaria tetraquetra

A. tetraquetra. The leaves are arranged in an unusual manner that are its only claim to fame. Best used as a dwarf carpeter. Tiny white flowers in May.

ARMERIA. Thrift. Form pleasing green cushions that look quite at home between large rocks. They do best in a light sandy soil in full sun. Increased by division early in the year. If attempted in the autumn, many of the pieces will rot off.

A. caespitosa. Beechwood. The aristocrat of the family. Little hummocks of grey-green narrow leaves. Large flower heads of silver pink on 4 in. stems in April.

A.c. 'Bevan's Variety'. Tight green cushions, deep pink flowers. May-June. 2 in.

A. corsica. The leaves are narrower than those of the ordinary Thrift. Flowers an unusual terra-cotta shade. Produces a succession of flowers from June till August. 6 in.

A. maritima. The native Sea Pink frequently found on our coast. The white form called 'alba' is also to be found. For garden work it is generally better to obtain one of the named hybrids, as the colours are uniform and stronger. May and June. 6 in.

ARNEBIA. 'Prophet Flower'.

A. echioides. An extraordinary plant. Sprays of bright primrose, each flower has five black spots, one on each petal. Well-drained soil in sun. May-June. 9-12 in.

ARTEMISIA. Wormwood aromatic herbs of a shrubby nature which need light sandy soil in full sun. Increased by heel cuttings in late summer.

A. pedemontana syn. lanata. Grown for its lovely silvergrey leaves which form a dense mound 3-6 in. deep, and makes a good contrast for deep coloured flowers growing near it. The flowers are not of any value and spoil the carpeting effect.

A. nutans. (A. argentea). Grey, scented foliage. 9 in.

A. schmidtiana 'Nana'. Creeping habit, silvery foliage. 6 in.

ASPERULA. Woodruff. Low-growing plants with narrow leaves. Most species prefer semi-shade. Increased by division or cuttings early in the year.

A. gussoni. Makes fat little green cushions covered with pink flowers in May. Does best in sun, but needs the deep root run provided by a scree.

A. lilaciflora caespitosa. Salmon pink on emerald mats.

A. suberosa. One of the favourite rock plants. The grey, woolly leaves need protection from winter damp. The flowers are clusters of delicate pink trumpets in June. 3 in.

ASTER. The dwarf Michaelmas Daisies can be used to good account in the rock garden as well as many other species of the family. All need a good garden soil to flower well, and the stronger growers benefit from frequent division.

A. alpinus. Purple daisy flowers in May and June. 6 in.

A.s. 'Albus'. Pure white.

A.a. 'Beechwood'. Erect large blue flowers.

A.a. 'Wargrave'. Magnificent. Large silvery pinky-mauve like daisies.

A. diplotephioides. Strong basal rosette of dark green leaves. The large purple flowers with distinct yellow eye are borne singly on 9 in. stems in June.

A. natalensis. Bright blue daisies. Unusual colours. Summer. 4-6 in.

A. souliei. Purple-violet with orange centre. Attractive. Summer. 6 in.

ASARINA. Snapdragon. The only one that is commonly grown in rock gardens, needs very well-drained positions in rock crevices. Is easily raised from seed.

A. procumbens. Prostrate spreading stems with ivy-shaped leaves. The flowers which are like those of the bedding Antirrhinum are borne singly along the stem and are clear citron yellow. Flowers all summer. Not always hardy, but easily raised from seed, self-sown seedlings often appear in the very places they look best, such as cracks in a large rock, where planting is almost impossible.

AUBRIETIA. Purple Rock Cress. One of the most universally grown of all rock plants. To be seen at its best, a position in full sun is needed, and the soil should be light and well-drained, containing lime. To keep the plants looking neat for many years, it is necessary to cut them back. This should be done directly after flowering. Do not be afraid to cut them hard – they will look quite bare for a couple of weeks and then make nice green mounds for winter, instead of the straggling patches so often seen. For ordinary purposes, division will give enough plants, but cuttings can also be taken. Named varieties are many, and a good strain of seed will provide many worthwhile colours, from which the best should be selected. Never waste good space on bad plants when there are so many beautiful ones from which to choose.

'Bressingham Pink'. Clear pink, double.

'Crimson King'. Large, red purple.

'Dr. Mules'. Dark blue purple.

'Gloriosa'. Very large, rose pink.

'Godstone'. Deep purple.

'*Greencourt Purple*'. Vigorous, double purple flowers over a long period.

'*Hartswood Purple*'. Very vigorous, deep purple.

'*Joan Allen*'. Large flowered, double, crimson.

'*Lavender Gem*'. Compact variety. Produces blooms galore.

'*Lloyd Edwards*'. Deep violet.

'*Lodge Crave*'. Semi-double; violet-blue.

'*Mrs. Rodewald*'. Rich crimson.

'*Red Carnival*'. Good strong red.

'*Stock Flowered Pink*'. Double, pink.

'*Wanda*'. Double, red.

A. *variegata argentea*. Leaves beautifully marked with white, very neat growth. Flowers pale mauve.

'*Vindictive*'. Good strong crimson. Very vigorous grower.

BELLIS. Daisy. Though not the correct type of plant for the rock garden, few people can resist putting in a patch here and there to give a little extra colour. They are greedy plants and need a good rich soil to look well. Easily increased by division and some come true from seed.

'*Dresden China*'. Miniature pale pink buttons.

'*Rob Roy*'. Deep red, double flowers.

BELLIUM. Suitable as a little carpeter that will not swamp small plants. Will grow in ordinary light soil and is increased by division.

B. *minutum*. White daisy flowers which fade through pink to red are produced all summer. 1 in.

CALAMINTHA. A charming little plant of shrubby growth with aromatic leaves, rather like the Thymes, but with much larger flowers. Light sandy soil and full sun are needed. Cuttings in pure sand in spring root quite easily, but plants from seed are a better shape.

C. *alpina*. Purple flowers in June. A neat growing little bush. 6 in.

CALCEOLARIA. Need a soil that does not dry out during the summer, yet must not be waterlogged in winter. Partial shade, but away from the drip from trees or shrubs.

C. *biflora*. Pouches of yellow flowers over dark green rosettes. Summer. 4-6 in.

C. *polyrrhiza syn. acutifolia*. Spreads by creeping under ground roots. Flowers deep yellow on 6 in. stems that rise from the mat of leaves. July.

C. tenella. Bright green carpet in semi-shade. If planted beside a large rock, it will quickly spread to cover the whole area, and the part that is on bare rock will survive a hard winter better than in soil. Yellow flowers lightly speckled with crimson. 2 in.

CALOCEPHALUS. 'The Aluminium Plant'.

C. brownii. Silver shrub, button-like flowers. 9 in.

CAMPANULA. Bell Flower. Invaluable plants for many purposes, they do best in a good well-drained soil, with a little leaf mould added. They prefer a sunny position, but some will make a good show in the semi-shade also. Most of them spread by underground shoots and the clumps can be divided in spring when growth has started. Some are best raised from seed, but named varieties will not breed true. Only a selection of the very many species grown will be given here.

C. allionii. Prostrate plant best suited for the scree. Large, deep-blue purple bells. June to August. 3 in.

C. arvatica. A really dwarf species, best for scree or alpine house, as it gets lost among rampant plants. Upstanding, starry flowers of deep violet. 2 in.

C. cochlearifolia (pusilla). All these names are found in trade catalogues for the dwarf Harebell. Quite hardy, and able to stand the wear and tear of life in a paved walk. Small, lavender blue bells. 4 in.

C.c. 'Cambridge Blue'. Dainty light blue bells.

C.c. 'Miss Willmott'. Medium blue bells.

C.c. 'Oakington Blue'. Deep greyish-blue bells.

C. carpatica. Very easy to grow. Rather too large for the small rock garden, but excellent in a mixed flower border. Blue. 12 in. There are some very good named varieties which are not too tall.

C.c. alba. White form of above.

C. collina. Violet spikes. 9 in.

C. fenestrellata. Countless dainty lilac stars. Summer. 3 in.

C. garganica. Grows as a flat rosette which sends out prostrate stems covered with starry flowers over a long season, starting in June. 3 in.

C.g. 'Blue Diamond'. Dark blue stars. June. 3 in.

C.g. 'W. H. Paine'. A beautiful distinct variety. The bright violet blue flowers have clearly marked white centres.

C.g. 'G. F. Wilson'. Dense mats of foliage bearing large violet bells. July-August. 3-4 in.

C. glomerata 'Acaulis'. Rich violet flowers in the foliage. June - August. 6 in.

C.g. 'Acaulis Alba'. A beautiful white.

C. Innesii. Light purple, violet-centred, wide open bells. July-August. 6 in.

C. kemulariae. Violet-purple. Glossy foliage. July. 6 in.

C. kewensis. A beautiful miniature hybrid which is best grown in a pan in the alpine house. Dark blue, starry flowers. 3 in.

C.k. 'Mist Maiden'. Looks like a cloud of white mist.

C. nitida alba. Dark shiny leaves. Stiff, erect stems 9 in. high with pure white flowers in July. Must be lifted and replanted frequently, as they tend to wear themselves out with much flowering. Increase by planting out young side shoots singly into good soil.

C. portenschlagiana (muralis). The most useful of all the campanulas. Will flower in sun or semi-shade in almost any soil. The trailing spikes of violet blue bells are produced all through the summer and far into the autumn. 6 in.

C. poscharskyana. Makes strong clumps of green leaves. The flowers are lavender blue stars borne on long trailing red stems. Excellent on a wall where the flower stems press against the stone and radiate in all directions covering a large area. Summer into autumn. 8 in.

C.p. 'Lisduggan'. Pink flowered.

C.p. 'Stella'. Dainty deep-blue stars.

C. persicifolia. 'Planiflora'. Stiff spikes of porcelain blue glossy rosettes. June. 6-8 in.

C. pulla. A beautiful little plant with pendulous blooms of metallic purple, that are very large for the size of the plant. Good for the scree or alpine house. June and July. 3 in.

C. punctata. Attractive. Spikes of enormous white bells flushed purple. June-July. 12-18 in.

C. raineri. Large, blue cups on very short stems, leaves grey green. June and July.

C. rotundifolia. The native Harebell, a good form with deep blue flowers is well worth a place in the garden.

C. sarmatica. Erect with lavender-mauve bells. Downy leaves. Summer. 12 in.

C. stansfieldii. A hybrid with pale green leaves that form a loose mat. The flowers are clear lavender and have very pointed teeth edging the narrow bell. 4 in.

C. turbinata. (Syn. *carpatica*). Hairy, greyish leaves. Large, blue flowers. Summer. 9 in. Like a dwarfer, C. carpatica.

C.t. albescens. A silvery blue counterpart of the above. The two are very effective when planted together.

C. warleyensis. Double flowers of china blue. July and August. 6 in. The stems are not strong enough to hold the flowers erect when they are heavy after rain, so a good layer of limestone chippings or gravel will help to keep the flowers from getting muddied.

CARDUNCELLUS. A hardy plant for sunny positions.

C. pinnatus acaulis. Cut leaves, blue heads nestling in foliage. July-August.

C. rhaponticoides. Rosettes of violet-blue powder-puffs. July-August. 2 in.

CASSINIA. 'The Golden Heather'.

C. fulvida. Crowded golden leaves, fluffy seed heads. 3 ft.

CELMISIA.

C. bellidioides. Glossy leaves with white daisies. Peaty soil, sun. Early summer. 3 in.

CENTAUREA. One of the Cornflowers.

C. simplicaulis. Rosy flowers and silvery foliage. June-July. 4-6 in.

CARLINA. A dwarf Thistle that should be planted in very poor soil or it will become too rampant. Interesting because it figures in very many of the designs for carving and embroidery found in alpine districts.

C. acaulis. A flat rosette of prickly leaves with a large, stemless flower in the centre. June.

CERASTIUM. Snow in Summer. A very rampant grower that must be cut back drastically after flowering to keep it within bounds. Any light soil will do for it, and in full sun it is covered with flower. Divide the plants when they become too straggly.

C. biebersteinii. Greyish leaves. White flowers in May. 6 in.

C. lanatum. Choice plant. Leaves very woolly with white flowers, very compact.

CHEIRANTHUS. Wallflower. The ones suited for the rock garden are neater growing than the well known bedding wallflower. They need well-drained soil that contains lime, and a sunny position. Though really perennials, it is best to keep a succession of young plants coming on, as they are very liable to get eelworm. Should this appear, the infected plants must be pulled up at once and burned. If you are an experienced composter the plants can be composted.

> C. 'Harpur Crewe'. Double golden yellow flowers in spring. 15 in. If cut back after flowering, will give a second crop of bloom.

Chrysanthemum hosmariense

> C. 'Moonlight'. Clear lemon yellow. 9 in.
>
> C. mutabilis. Flowers mixed bronze and purple. 9 in.
>
> C. rufus. Beautiful fiery red-orange. 9 in.

CHRYSANTHEMUM. Most of the family are too closely associated with greenhouses and florists to be 'right' in the rock garden, but two in particular deserve a place.

> C. haradjanii. The silver leaf is like the feather of a bird. Any soil. Sun. 4-6 in.
>
> C. hosmariense. Handsome foliage and white flowers always in bloom.

CHRYSOGONUM. 'The Golden Knee'. A peculiar name for a lovely plant.

> C. virginianum. A succession of yellow flowers. Any soil. Sun. Summer. 6-9 in.

CHRYSOPSIS. Compositae. One of the very big daisy family.

C. *villosa*. Yellow daisies on greyish foliage. Summer. 6 in.

CODONOPSIS. Related to the Campanulas, but with a long, fleshy root. Grow it in light soil in full sun. Much beloved by slugs in spring. Easily raised from seed.

C. *ovata*. Prostrate stems bearing pale blue bells, the inside of which are marked with dark veins.

CONVOLVULUS. Bindweed. Beware of these – any with fat, white roots should be left for the owners of very large gardens. Beautiful no doubt, but they just cannot be kept within bounds. The shrubby ones are safe, but rather delicate.

C. *cneorum*. Shrubby with silver leaves. Large, pink flowers. 18 in.

C. *mauretanicus*. Trailing stems of periwinkle blue flowers July to September. 9 in. In a well-drained soil protected from hard winter weather, this will survive many seasons.

COREOPSIS. Compositae. Any soil in a sunny spot.

C. *lanceolata*. 'Sunny Boy'. Masses of yellow flowers. Summer. 6-9 in.

C. 'Sunchild'. A new introduction, yellow flowers marked red towards the centre. Summer. 6-9 in.

CORETHROGENE. Compositae. Like Chrysopsis a typical daisy – but very pretty.

C. *californicum*. Bears pink daisies on grey foliage. Loves gritty soil. Summer. 6-8 in.

CORYDALIS. Fumitory. These plants have a deceptively delicate appearance for in reality they are very sturdy. Good ordinary soil, will thrive in sun or half-shade. Increase bulbous species by division, others by seed.

C. *solida*. The ferny leaves have a grey-blue tinge which make a good colour scheme with the mauve pink flowers in April. 6 in. The whole plant dies down after flowering till the following season.

CREPIS. A dainty little plant – grows in any soil. Loves the sun.

C. *incana*. Masses of bright pink dandelion flowers. Sun. Summer. 6-9 in.

CYANANTHUS. Not very easy to grow. They need a lime-free soil, and that difficult combination of a plentiful supply of moisture in summer while being well drained in winter.

Protect from slugs. Cuttings taken early in the year give the best results.

> *C. lobatus.* Leaves larger and a deeper green. Flowers dark blue.

> *C. microphyllus.* Hardiest and best. Powder blue. Good for scree or sunk garden.

CYNOGLOSSUM. Hound's Tongue. Best raised from seed every second year, as the plants are not very long lived. Full sun and well drained soil.

> *C. nervosum.* Greyish leaves. Flowers like a large Forget-me-not of the most intense blue. In another more usual colour, the plant would not be worth a place among the alpines, but coming as it does in late summer, it justifies the trouble of raising new plants frequently. 12 in.

DELPHINIUM. Of the many small-growing species listed in catalogues, few are really worth the trouble needed to protect them from the constant attacks of slugs. Good garden loam and a position in the sun. Increased by seed.

> *D. cashmerianum.* Dwarf, produces large blue-purple flowers. Summer. 9 in.

> *D. nudicaule.* 'Orange scarlet'. June and July. 12 in. Has fleshy root stocks. Disappears completely in winter.

DIANTHUS. Pink. Few families provide so many delightful and easy plants for the rock garden as the Dianthus. There is a large range of sizes and colours to be had, and varying types of growth to suit different positions. The soil should be gritty and contain lime, and the habit and flowering of the plants is best when they are in full sun. When a special named variety is wanted, increase by cuttings or division, but seed will give attractive mixtures from which the best can be selected for planting out.

> *Dianthus 'Grenadier'.* Neat little tufted plant. Very free flowering all through the summer. Scarlet, maroon. 4 in.

> *D. Mars* syn. *'Brigadier'.* As the above, but the flowers are a strong crimson.

> *D. Mrs. Clarke.* Bright large crimson. June and July. 9 in.

> *D. arvernensis.* Neat, low growing foliage, makes lovely cushions in a paving or on a wall. Small pink flowers in May and June. 3 in.

> *D. caesius.* The Cheddar Pink. This species and its many

hybrids are obliging plants that make good grey-green cushions and have flower stems 6 in. high. Flowers can be double or single, and the colour ranges from white through pink to deepest red.

D. deltoides. Comes true from seed and is best raised that way. The leaves are small and either green or reddish brown. Flowers strong pink with tiny flecks of crimson. Summer. 6 in.

D. myrtinervius. Neat green hummocks. Dainty pink flowers for scree or trough.

D. neglectus. Narrow green leaves. Flowers carmine with reverse of the petals buff. June and July. 4 in.

D. 'Pike's Pink'. Double pink, scented, free flowering. Summer. 4 in.

D. squarrosus. Pure white, deeply lacinated flowers on neat grey-green hummocks; sweetly scented. 6 in. May-July.

D. 'Waithman's Beauty'. Deep ruby-crimson flecked white. Summer. 8 in. Some of the garden hybrids usually grown in the flower border can be included, but avoid any that have heavy formal growth.

DIASCIA. Scrophulariaceae. Comes from Basutuland – loves the sun.

D. cordata. Cushions of dark glossy leaves plus spurred pink flowers. Must have good drainage.

DIMORPHOTHECA. A daisy-like plant – lots of sun please.

D. ecklonis prostrata. Flowers white above and purple beneath, conspicuous blue-violet ring inside. Summer. 6-9 in.

DORONICUM. The Leopard's Bane of the garden. Easy to grow in any soil.

D. cordatum. Golden like daisies. May. 6 in.

DOUGLASIA. Makes cushions of grey-green shoots like miniature fir trees. Well-drained deep sandy soil in full sun. Increase by cuttings or seed.

D. vitaliana. Heads of golden flowers in spring. 3 in. Suitable for the scree.

DRABA. Whitlow Grass. A race of rather dull little plants which look too near the borderline of being weak-growing weeds to be popular. Sandy soil in full sun. Seed or division.

D. aizoides. Green, thorny looking rosettes. Golden yellow flowers in spring. 3 in.

D. bruniifolia. Cushions like moss plus yellow flowers. April-June. 2 in.

D. rigida. Green carpets plus yellow flowers. May. 2 in.

DRYAS. Mountain avens. Useful for the good carpet of strong green leaves as well as the flowers and attractive seed heads. Sandy soil in sun or semi-shade. Increase by cuttings or division.

D. octopetala minor. White flowers with golden anthers from June to August, followed by fluffy seed heads. 2 in.

D.o. suendermannii. Oak-like leaves. Pure white flower. Golden stemmed cups. Pretty seed pods. Summer. 4 in.

EDRAIANTHUS. Wahlenbergia. Closely allied to the Campanulas. They need a well-drained, stony soil and a sunny position. Increased by seed and cuttings. Keep a watch out for slugs, specially if seed is to be saved – the slugs seem to like to eat the whole of the seed case before it ripens.

E. graminifolius. Large blue Campanula-like flowers in clusters. May-September. 3 in.

E. serpyllifolius major. Slender prostrate stems, ending in large, satiny upturned bells. May. Lovely in the scree or in pans.

E. tenuifolius. Narrow grey leaves. Pale lavender bells on slender stems. June.

EOMECON. One of the baby poppies.

E. chionanthum. White, gold centred flowers. Glaucous foliage. Likes a shady position. Loves sedge peat. Spring and summer. 8 in.

EPILOBIUM. Willow Herb. There is one member of this family of strong growing herbs, of which the Rose Bay is the best known, that is suitable for the rock garden. Stony soil, rich in humus, and an ample supply of moisture is needed for the plant to spread happily. Sun or semi-shade. Can be increased by division in spring, cuttings or seed.

E. fleischeri. Useful because it flowers in August. Soft pink and claret.

E. glabellum. Bronzy foliage, creamy white flowers.

ERIGERON. Fleabane. Aster-like plants, the low growing ones being suitable for the rock garden, and even those generally planted in the flower borders can be used where space allows. Ordinary garden soil in sun. Division or seed.

E. *aurantiacus.* A dwarf little daisy. Pastel orange flowers. June-July. 9 in.

E. *flettii* 'Foerster's Liebling'. Bears double deep cerise-pink flowers with finely cut petals. Lovely. Summer. 9-12 in.

E. *roylei.* Erect neat habit. Clear lilac, about 6 in.

ERINUS. The perfect little plant for the rock garden or seeding itself on old walls. Light, poor soil and full sun are needed to get the best results. If grown in rich soil, many of the plants will die in the winter through bad drainage. Seed; named varieties will not come true when planted near other forms, with which they cross freely.

E. *alpinus.* Neat little rosette of leaves and spikes of flowers growing from 3-6 in. high, according to the situation. Mauvish pink.

E.a. *albus.* A white form of the above.

E.a. *Abbottswood Pink.* A pretty clear pink.

E. a. *Dr. Hanaele.* Rich ruby red.

ERODIUM. *Stork's Bill.* While never making a blaze of colour, these plants give a steady succession of bloom over a long period. The whole plant is generally attractive in its type of growth, and the foliage is aromatic. They thrive in light, sandy soil and do best in full sun. Increased by seeds or cuttings.

E. *chamaedryoides roseum.* (syn. *reichardii roseum*). Flat rosettes of small green leaves. Covered all summer with pink, starry flowers. 2 in.

E. *chrysanthum.* Ferny, grey green leaves. Pale yellow flowers. June-September. 6 in.

E. *corsicum.* Round leaves with scalloped edges. Pale pink flowers in summer. 4 in.

E. *macradenum.* (syn. *petraeum glandulosum*). Ferny foliage. Pink flowers with dark blotches on the lower petals. 6 in.

E. *guttatum.* Fern-like foliage. White flowers marked with chocolate. Summer. 6 in.

ERYSIMUM. Much confusion exists in the naming of these plants, the simplest method is to realize that they are often classed with the Cheiranthus, and leave the Botanists to worry about the slight differences that divide them. Light soil containing lime and a sunny position are all they need. Raise new plants by seed or cuttings to replace those that have become too woody or straggling with age.

E. linifolium. Wiry plant with narrow leaves, and covered with lilac flowers in summer. 9 in.

E. pumilum (syn. *helveticum*). Tufted grey-green growth with yellow flowers, scented. 4 in.

ERYTHRAEA. Centaury. Centaurium. A lime-hating plant that does well planted among Gentians. Well-drained peat soil. Increased by division or seed.

E. scilloides diffusa. Compact leaves yellowish green. Flowers clean pink in June to October. 3 in.

EURYOPS. A daisy-like plant, like a Senecio. Likes a well-drained soil.

E. acraeus. (*E. evansii*). Very attractive. Silvery foliage and gamboge-yellow flowers. Plant in the sun. May-June. 6-9 in.

FRANKENIA. Sea Heath. Used for paving and the sides of paths. The foliage is small and heath-like. Easily increased by planting out the rooted shoots which spread all round the plant. Loves the sun and light soil.

F. thymifolia. Grey-green mats, bears pretty tiny pink flowers. June-August. 1 in.

GAILLARDIA. Another daisy-like flowering plant. Easy to grow anywhere. Likes sun.

G. nana Nieske. Dwarf, bears yellow and red flowers. Summer. 6-8 in.

GAZANIA. Not alpines and not quite hardy, yet these brilliant plants seem to be claiming a place in rock gardens of the present day. They are natives of South Africa, and combine long flowering with a full range of fiery colours. Very sunny positions in light, sandy soil give them the best chance of coming through the winter. Cuttings root very easily in sand, and many interesting hybrids can be raised from seed.

G. splendens. Trailing habit. Brilliant orange, the centre is marked with black and white arranged in a regular pattern.

Many named hybrids in shades of red, yellow, orange and deep bronze. Nearly all have the centre of the large daisy flowers marked with darker colours often in combination with pure white.

GENTIANA. Of the very many Gentians that have been introduced into this country, only a specialist would want

sophila. Light, sandy soil and full sun. Comes easily from cuttings taken in early summer.

G. fratensis. Makes large hummocks of pale green leaves. Clear pink flowers in June and July. 3 in.

G. repens. So like the above that many nurserymen list them as the same plant.

G.r. 'Letchworth Rose'. Deep pink flowers, trailing foliage. May-August. 4-6 in.

G.r. 'Rosea'. Pale pink form. Summer. 4-6 in.

HABERLEA. Plants for the cool side of a rock, needing lime-free soil and protection from winter damp. Side shoots pulled from the old plant will root quickly, or leaf cuttings can be taken.

H. rhodopensis. Rosettes of thick, green leaves. Sprays of mottled, lilac flowers in May. 6 in.

HALIMIUM. Cistaceae.

H. commutatum (Helianthemum rosmarinifolium). Rosemary-like leaves, yellow flowers. Any soil, full sun.

HAPLOPAPPUS — Compositae.

H. coronopifolius. Golden daisies, dark green rosette-like leaves. In sun, any soil. May-Sepember. 6 in.

HEBE. The shrubby counterparts of Veronicas. Grow in any soil in sun or part shade. Come from New Zealand.

H. buchananii 'Minor'. A mini shrub with tight neat leaves. 2-3 in.

H.x. edinensis. Yellowy green foliage plus white flowers. 3-6 in.

H. lavaudiana. Neat evergreen with white spikes. May. 6 in.

H. pimeleoides. Evergreen, small glaucous leaves. Violet-blue. July-August. 6-8 in.

HELIANTHEMUM. Rock Rose, Sun Rose. An invaluable dwarf shrub with large flowers of many shades. Light soil and full sun suit it best. Cut the plants back hard each year, directly after flowering and they will not get straggly. Increase by cuttings, seed also grows, but generally gives rather a large number of poor forms.

H. alpestre. A neat growing species with prostrate shoots of small, shiny leaves. Bright yellow flowers. June. 2 in.

H. lunulatum. Grey-green leaves on stiff, woody little stems that make an erect little shrub about 4 in. high, excellent for planting in a trough garden, or to give height in a bowl planted up as a miniature rock garden. Yellow flowers in great profusion in July.

H. nummularium. These are many, the double-flowered ones hold longer, but do not give nearly such a blaze of colour.

H.n. Ben Alder. Terra cotta.

H.n. 'Butter and Eggs'. Double yellow flowers with orange towards centre.

H.n. 'Chocolate Blotch'. Orange petals, spotted brown. Grey leaves.

H.n. 'Ben Lomond'. Rose Madder.

H.n. 'Ben Nevis'. Yellow with orange eye.

H.n. 'Raspberry Ripple'. Deep pink, flecked white.

H.n. 'Rose of Leeswood'. Fine double pink.

H.n. 'Supreme'. Glowing crimson, long flowering.

H. rosmarinifolium. (syn. *Halimium commentatum*). (See under Halimium.)

HELICHRYSUM. Everlasting Flower. Well-drained soil in sun, though some will do in semi-shade. Spreads quickly, carpeting the ground with small leaves, divide the plants in early spring.

H. bellidioides. Rampant carpeter, White flowers. 6 in.

H. lanatum. Grey woolly foliage. Brilliant yellow flowers. Attractive. Summer. 6-8 in.

H. milfordiae. Silver leaves, russet-pink Everlasting flowers. May. 3 in.

H. virginianum. Silvery leaves, pinkish buds turning to creamy white, for pan, or scree, charming.

HERACLEUM. Umbelliferae.

H. minimum 'Roseum'. Looks like a miniature pink 'Cow Parsley'. In sun, well-drained soil. Summer. 6 in.

HEUCHERA. Really best in the flower garden, but where space can be found for a few of the red ones, they are a great help in providing colour in the later part of the summer, when things look rather drab. Rich garden soil. Side shoots pulled off and rooted in sand, make better shaped plants than ordinary division of roots.

H. Pluie de Feu. Crimson red.

H. sanguinea. Scarlet red, half shade. June-July. 15 in.

HIERACIUM. Hawk Weed. Watch out that they don't spread too far. Any ordinary soil.

H. aurantiacum. Heads of deep orange red Dandelion flowers. Spreads very rapidly.

H. villosum. Leaves covered with long, white hairs which

make the whole plant pale grey. Flowers like large Dandelions of lemon yellow. A striking plant, but too free in setting seed.

HORMINUM. Labiatae.

    H. pyrenaicum. Crinkly green rosettes. Bright purple-blue flowers. In sun or part shade. Any soil. Summer. 6-8 in.

HOUSTONIA. Bluets. A tiny plant with low green foliage that makes a 'lawn', if planted in leafy soil that does not dry up during the summer. Needs to be replanted most years.

    H. coerulea. Little blue flowers on 2-in. stems in May and at intervals during the season.

HUTCHINSIA. A bright green carpeter that stays 1 in. high. Cool soil in partial shade.

    H. alpina. Finely cut leaves, like cress. Heads of tiny white flowers in May.

HYDRANGEA. Saxifragaceae. A member of the Saxifrage family.

    H. 'Pia'. Remarkable baby, very dwarf. Large rich red heads. A well-drained soil plus peat. No lime. Summer. 6 in.

HYPERICUM. St. John's Wort. A really useful genus. Even the dullest have some claim to beauty, and most are neat growing. Light soil in a sunny position. Most of them come true from seed and are most easily raised that way.

    H. aegypticum. A fine-leaved little bushlet, bearing golden flowers all summer. 6 in.

    H. empetrifolium prostratum. Prostrate, woody stems, covered with bright yellow flowers in summer. 2 in. Lovely in the scree or alpine house.

    H. inodorum 'Elstead'. Dwarf yellow flowers, attractive red seed pods. Summer. Cut back each Spring.

    H. fragile. Cut back each year after flowering, this bushlet remains neat for many years. Large, golden yellow flowers June till September. 9 in. Older plants up to 15 in.

    H. olympicum. Flowers like the above, but type of growth less dense.

    H.o. sulphureum. A lemon yellow form of the above.

    H. patulum 'Hidcote'. Large golden yellow bowl-like flowers.

H. reptans. Trailing. Best in semi-shade where it keeps moist. Large, yellow flowers. 3 in.

H. trichocaulon. Bears sheets of bronzy-red buds plus golden flowers. July-August. 2-3 in.

HYPSELLA. A low-growing plant which spreads rapidly by underground stems (provided the slugs don't find it first!) and is useful as a carpeter in sun or semi-shade. Good soil with plenty of humus. Increase by division of roots in spring.

H. longiflora. Shiny, green leaves. Striped purplish pink and white. All summer. 1 in.

IBERIS. Candytuft. Very useful plant, forming evergreen mounds that look well all the year round. Any ordinary garden soil suits them. Will thrive equally well on walls, in paving or in the border. Increase by cuttings or seed.

I. gibraltarica. Rather disappointing as it gets very leggy. Flowers in varying shades of purple and mauve. Select only the best colours from a batch of seedlings. 6 in.

I. sempervirens. Little Gem. Makes a neat little bush. Heads of white flowers in May and June. 6 in.

I.s. Snowflake. Larger than the above in every way. Needs to be cut back every year to keep it compact. Large white flowers in April and May that completely conceal the leaves, and transform the plant into a sheet of the purest white. 12 in.

I. ventricosus. Mat forming. Bears white heads early summer. 3-4 in.

INULA. Another herbaceous plant that is small enough to find a home in the rock garden. Good garden soil, sunny position. Divide when the plants get overcrowded.

I. ensifolia. Narrow, pointed leaves. Large, yellow daisy flowers. July to September. 9 in.

IRIS. As well as the dwarf bulbous Irises, there are a few that are a great asset in the rock garden. Well-drained soil in full sun is needed for the species mentioned here.

I. cristata. A dwarf, much beloved by slugs. Blue flowers marked with gold. April and May. 3 in. Best for scree or alpine house.

I. forrestii. Yellow flowers veined brown. Early summer. 15 in.

I. graminea. Purple-blue falls and a rosy-red centre. Attractive. June. 12 in.

I. pumila. Like the large Germanica Iris, except for its size. There are many named varieties all excellent for the rock garden, in shades of blue, yellow, purple and white. April. Heights vary from 3-12 in.

I.p. 'Amber Queen'. Coppery yellow.

I.p. 'Azurea'. Stemless blue flowers.

I.p. 'Cyanea'. Fine dwarf purple.

I.p. 'Lutea'. Pale yellow.

I.p. 'Violacea'. Ruby purple and pale blue.

I. setosa. Purplish-blue, mottled. Charming. May-June. 6 in.

JASIONE. Sheep's-head Scabious. Grown in poor, light soil where it stays dwarf. The flowers make a blue haze which is attractive between patches of Rock roses. Seeds itself freely, but does not become a nuisance.

J. perennis. Powder blue flower heads in June. Height varies with the position. 4-12 in.

LAPEYROUSIA. A member of the Iris family.

L. laxa. A bulbous plant with carmine and orange sprays. Warm sunny spot. Summer. 6 in.

LAVANDULA. One of the Lavenders. Will grow in any soil in the sun.

L. stoechas. A French Lavender. Unusual type. Bears inflated purple heads. Most attractive. July-August. 9-12 in.

LEONTOPODIUM. Edelweiss. A plant from the high Alps. Contrary to popular opinion, it is quite easy to grow.

Edelweiss, Leontopodium alpinum

Well-drained soil in a sunny position is all it requires.
Once established, leave it alone to grow into a large plant.

>   *L. alpinum.* Produces the well known Flannel Flowers
>   from June till August. 6 in.

LEPTOSPERMUM. One of the myrtles – loves a sunny
spot.

>   *L. scoparium 'Nanum'.* A delightful dwarf. Small, dark
>   green leaves and round pink flowers. Alpine house.
>   6 in.

LEWISIA. These plants come from America, where they
grow in the hot, dry districts of California. To succeed here
they must have a light, sandy soil, plenty of water in the
growing season, all the sun available and dry conditions
during the dormant season. All this is naturally most easily
provided in the alpine house, where they are seen at their
best. Very favoured gardens will be able to give the right
conditions, but on the whole, the results are disappointing.
Freshly saved seed germinates very well, and the strongest
plants will flower in their second season, though the size of
bloom will improve in subsequent years.

>   *L. columbiana.* Narrow leaves. Umbels of small, pink
>   flowers. May. 6 in.
>   *L. howelli.* Like the above in growth. Flowers striped
>   pink and apricot. May and June.
>   *L. rediviva.* Upright, narrow leaves which die down after
>   flowering season. Flowers are large and cup-shaped
>   on 2-in. stems, and vary in colour from white to pink.
>   *L. nevadensis.* Lop-sided white flowers, veined green.
>   Dormant in late summer. For scree or alpine house.
>   1-2 in. May-June.

LIMONIUM. One of the Statices or Sea Lavender.
Grows in any good soil. Loves the sun.

>   *L. minutum.* Charming rich lavender flowers. August-
>   September. 4-6 in.

LINARIA. Toadflax. Beware of these plants – they look
so small and delicate, but the ones that spread by underground stems are as vigorous and determined invaders as
the worst weeds. Light, sandy soil, and a position where
they may seed at will is best for the following species, all
of which can be kept under control.

>   *L. alpina.* Trailing stems with narrow, grey leaves. Little
>   snapdragon flowers of violet and orange. May to July.
>   3 in.

L.a. rosea. Flowers pink and orange.

L. cymbalaria 'Globosa'. Green hummocks with tiny mauve Snapdragon-like flowers. Summer. 2-3 in.

L.c. 'Globosa Rosea'. A pink Globosa.

L. origanifolia. Leaves hairy. Upright growth. Flowers are large for the size of the stems. Purple and mauve. Summer. 6 in.

L. pilosa (syn. L. pollida). Lavender and yellow flowers constantly in bloom. Summer. 6 in.

LINUM. Flax. This family provides some beautiful clean colours that are very welcome when planning a colour scheme. Well-drained loam and a sunny position. Seed where possible, but cuttings of L. arboreum.

L. arboreum. Neat little bush, covered with large, clear yellow flowers in May till July. 12 in. Will also grow in semi-shade.

L. flavum. Flowers like the above. The stems should be cut down each year. June. 15 in. Really more suitable for the herbaceous border.

L. narbonense. Tall, waving stems bearing huge flowers of deep blue all summer. 15 in. Be sure to get a good coloured strain. The Six Hills variety is excellent.

L. perenne alpinum. Prostrate little blue flax. May and June. 2 in.

L. suffruticosum salsoloides 'Nanum'. Grey-green leaves plus pearly opalescent flowers. Summer. 2 in.

LIPPIA. One of the Verbenas often called 'Vervain'. Grows in any soil. Likes the sun.

L. canescens (syn. repens). Little creeping plant. Produces masses of pinky-mauve Scabious-like flowers. Summer. 1 in.

LITHOSPERMUM. Gromwell. Small, woody plants that dislike lime. Cuttings put in early in the year give the best results.

L. graminifolium. Long narrow, dark-green leaves. Flower heads are clusters of drooping bells of clear blue. May. 6 in.

L. intermedium. Type of growth like the above, but the full-grown bush is taller.

L. prostratum (syn. diffusum). Continuous succession of brilliant blue flowers along the trailing stems. Will thrive in peat or in a heavy loam, provided it is free of lime.

L.p. 'Heavenly Blue'. Glorious sheets of blue.

LOBELIA.

> *L. syphilitica.* Bright blue flowers borne late. August-September. 9-12 in.

LYCHNIS. Catchfly. Obliging little plants that will grow in almost any soil. Come freely from seed, except the double flowered forms, which must be propagated by cuttings.

> *L. alpina.* A dull little plant which looks best in large groups. Puce pink in Spring. 4 in.
>
> *L. flos-jovis.* 'Horts Var'. Silky rosettes plus light crimson heads. Summer. 12 in.
>
> *L.x. haageana.* Strain of brilliant flowers 2 in. across, in scarlet, crimson and salmon. Summer. 9 in.
>
> *L. viscaria flore pleno.* Free flowering, strong pink. May and June. 12 in. The single form is a poor thing, though the variety splendens is a good colour.

LYSIMACHIA. Creeping Jenny. This little creeper will really grow anywhere, even in city gardens. Used in the ordinary rock garden, care must be taken that it does not over-run nearby plants, as it grows very quickly.

> *L. nummularia.* Carpet of green leaves studded with bright yellow flowers from June till September. 1 in.
>
> *L.n. aurea.* A golden-leaved form that is not quite so vigorous.

MALVASTRUM. One of the Mallows, likes lots of sun.

> *M. lateritium.* Deep pink flowers suffused orange. 6 in.

MAZUS. Low-growing carpeter, useful for paving in a cool, moist situation. Increases quickly and can be divided in spring.

> *M. reptans.* Flowers large for the size of the plant. Pale violet with large golden spot on the petals. May until Autumn. 1 in.

MENTHA. Mint. Only one species will be included here, the majority being unsuitable for rock gardens.

> *M. requienii.* A close little carpeter that smells strongly of Peppermint when touched. It spreads quickly over the soil in a cool, moist place. Sometimes looks rather sad after a hard winter, but soon greens up again. The flowers are like mauve pin-heads scattered all over the plant.

MORISIA. Needs a gritty soil of considerable depth, where its long tap root can penetrate in search of moisture.

The leaves lie flat on the ground, and the whole plant looks just like a green starfish. Propagation is done by putting root cuttings into pure sand.

M. *hypogœoa* (syn. *monantha*). Yellow flowers in spring. 1 in. Useful in the scree.

MYOSOTIS. Forget-me-not. The ordinary Forget-me-not should be kept out of the rock garden. It is not a rock plant and cannot look like one. The three mentioned here are true perennials, and by their habit of growth can be used. Well-drained soil and hard treatment is needed. In rich soil they grow too soft. Propagate by seed.

M. *explanata.* Grey-green hairy leaves, white flowers yellow centred. Very neat.

M. *rupicola.* Flowers azure blue. Spring. 2 in.

M. *spathulata.* Unusual trailing stems. The flowers are pure white. 1 in.

NEPETA. Catmint. Too large for the small rock garden, but very useful in rock walls or bordering a paved path. Ordinary garden soil. The leaves are a better colour in a dry, sunny position. Cuttings of short basal shoots root quickly.

N. *mussini.* Grey-green leaves and long spikes of lavender flowers. Keep cut back every year.

There are named varieties with leaves or flowers of different size or colour, but they are seldom an improvement on N. mussini in length of flower or habit of growth.

OENOTHERA. Evening Primrose. These are numerous, but only a few are suitable for the rock garden. Light soil is best, and increase is by seed or cuttings, according to the species.

O. *glaber.* Bronzy-green leaves, buds red; yellow flowers. June-August. 12 in.

O. *missouriensis.* Rather coarse growing. The huge pale yellow flowers are stemless and produced in succession along the prostrate shoots, which look beautiful trailing over a sunny bank.

O. *perennis* (syn. *pumila*). Small yellow flowers. Summer. 6 in.

O. *tetragona riparia.* A beautiful plant. From a small rosette of basal leaves, long wiry stems grow to about 1 ft. high. These produce many large, yellow flowers all through the summer and early autumn. In windy places, it is advisable to put a few short, twiggy sticks around the plants, to prevent the brittle stems from being broken.

OMPHALODES. The species mentioned need different treatment and are better described separately.

O. cappadocica. A sturdy plant that thrives in sun or shade, is not fussy about soil, though prefers it cool and leafy, and as well as having a main flowering season in spring, will give occasional blossoms in autumn. Brilliant blue flowers, like large Forget-me-nots. 9 in.

O. luciliae. Grey, smooth leaves. Flowers pale blue with a faint tinge of pink, the whole very like the flowers in a Dresden china Shepherdess' basket. 4 in. Keep in well-drained, gritty soil, or the leaves get too large. Does very well in the scree.

O. verna. Bright blue flowers, creeping stems. Like peaty soil, part shade and good drainage. Spring. 3 in.

O. verna alba. A similar plant with white flowers.

ONOSMA. Plants with leaves covered with stiff hairs, and clusters of tubular flowers on stems of varied heights. Sandy, well-drained soil in sunny positions. Seed gives sturdier plants. The seedlings should be put in their permanent quarters as young as possible, or potted and transferred from them, as they dislike root disturbance.

O. albo-roseum. The flowers are white with a pink mouth that turns deep red with age. 9 in.

O. echoides. Often called 'The Golden Drop'. Hairy foliage. Tubular yellow flowers. Summer. 9 in.

O. tauricum. Flowers strong yellow. 9 in.

ORIGANUM. Dittany. Dainty plants with hop-like flowers that need light soil in a sunny position. Increase by careful division in the spring.

O. dictamnus. Woolly, aromatic leaves. Drooping heads of rosy purple flowers in summer, and remaining till autumn. 6 in. Best grown in the scree.

O. hybridum. Like the above, but larger and sturdier. Flowers purple. 9 in.

O. vulgare 'Aureum'. Neat golden-yellow bushes. Sunny spot. 4-6 in.

OROBUS. Early-flowering plant like a small vetch. Light soil in the sun, though it will flower in semi-shade. Grows freely from seed.

O. vernus (syn. *Lathyrus vernus*). Flowers are shaded
blue and purple. April and May. 9 in.

OROSTACHYS. One of the Crassula family – most unusual.

O. spinosa (syn. *Cotyledon spinosa*). Tight spiny rosettes.
Likes a hot, well-drained spot. Summer. 3 in.

OXALIS. Wood Sorrel. Most of the members of this family that are grown in the rock garden form fleshy bulbs, but
as they are treated more like herbaceous subjects, they are
included here. Many of the innocent carpeters must be
looked upon with suspicion, for they multiply as rapidly
as the worst weed, and are more difficult to eradicate, but
a few are an addition to the beauty of paved walk or rock
crevice, so discrimination must be used.

O. adenophylla. Pretty grey-green leaves followed by
large, delicate pink flowers in May. 3 in.

Oxalis adenophylla

O. corniculata. Low-growing little plant that seeds itself
all over the place and can become a nuisance.

O. brasiliensis. Purple-red flowers with yellow throat.
May. 3 in.

O. chrysantha. Continuous clouds of buttercup yellow
flowers. 3-4 in.

O. enneaphylla 'minutaefolia'. Crinkled leaves. Large
pinky-white goblet-like flowers. Summer. 2 in.

O. floribunda. Shamrock-like leaves. Rich pink flowers
all summer. 6 in.

O. inops. Charming large deep pink flowers. 3 in.

O. lobata. Rich golden yellow flowers in summer. 2 in. Dies down in winter.

O. magellanica. A little creeper with white flowers. Does not spread seed, so should be used in preference to O. corniculata.

PAPAVER. Poppy. Only one species is worth growing, and that should be raised frequently from seed, as old plants get ugly and often die off suddenly. Poor well-drained soil is best, and full sun.

P. alpinum. In shades of yellow, apricot, pink and also white. 3 in. Lives longer if planted in the scree, and will seed itself about, though never becoming a nuisance.

P. myabeanum. Rosettes of grey, hairy foliage. Lovely lemon-yellow poppies. Summer. 3 in.

PAROCHETUS. A carpeter for damp places that spreads quickly. The leaves are like clover. Dig up a lump each winter and put it in a box in a cold greenhouse or frame. The main plant may come through all right, but a supply in reserve is a safeguard.

P. communis. Rampant creeper with brilliant blue flowers. Any soil, partial sheltered shade. Summer.

PARONYCHIA. (Caryophyliaceae). One of the best wall plants.

P. argentea. Hairy grey mats with papery white bracts. Sandy soil. In sun.

PENTSTEMON. The shrubby species, introduced from America, are the most useful for the rock garden. Light loam in a sunny position gives the best results. The presence of peat in the soil is an advantage for some species, but they are not particular. Increased by cuttings which root easily in a sand frame.

P. confertus. Spikes of creamy-yellow flowers. June-July. 4-6 in.

P. heterophyllus 'Blue Gem'. Producing spikes of blue and pink flowers. Summer. 9-12 in.

P. linariodes coloradense. A crawling greyish foliage. Sky blue flowers. 1 in.

P. pinifolius. Attractive pine-like leaves. Bright scarlet flowers. June-September. 4-6 in.

P. roezlii. Dwarf shrublet. Clear ruby red flowers in May and June. 6 in. Does well in the scree. Commercial stocks are very mixed.

P. *scouleri.* Upright bush covered with spikes of clear
lilac in May and June. 12 in.

P. *'Six Hills Hybrid'.* Shrubby growth of a spreading
habit. Rosy purple flowers. 6 in.

Pentstemon roezlii

PHLOX. Among the most useful plants for the rock garden. Most of them need a light, well-drained soil in full
sun, a few prefer semi-shade and a peat soil. The plants
send out shoots that root naturally, thus propagation consists of selecting rooted pieces. When large numbers are
required, unrooted slips are put in a sand frame.

P. *adsurgens.* Round, shiny leaves. Shell-pink flowers in
May. 3 in. Needs a gritty, peat soil, and protection
from slugs in spring.

P. *amoena variegata.* Low-growing, neat plant with
green and white foliage. Covered with heads of rose-
pink flowers in April and May. 4 in. Protect from slugs.

P. *carolina.* Showy corymbs of purplish pink. 9-12 in.
Early summer.

P. *douglasii.* Neat cushions of spiny leaves, covered with
stemless lilac stars in May. 2 in.

P.d. *'Boothman's Variety'.* Clear mauve, violet centre.
Very nice. 2 in.

P.d. *'Rosea'.* Silvery-pink, creeping.

P.d. *'May Snow'.* White sheets. 2 in.

P. *stolonifera*. Round leaves. Spreads by long runners. Rose pink flowers in April. Leafy soil in semi-shade. 6 in.

P. *subulata*. The best known of the family, often called Rock Phlox. There are many named varieties in different colours.

Phlox subulata 'Fairy', growing in a wall

P.s. *'Betty'*. Pink. Largish flowers.

P.s. *'Greencourt Seedling'*. Mauve with deeper eye.

P.s. *'G. F. Wilson'*. Mauve blue.

P.s. *'Margery'*. Good pink.

P.s. *'Samson'*. Rose pink with red eye.

P.s. *'Sensation'*. Carmine-pink flowers.

PHYTEUMA. An unusual plant with horned flowers.

P. *sieberi*. Horned bright-blue flowers. Must be well-drained soil in sun. Summer. 6 in.

PIMELEA. A daphne from New Zealand. A baby shrub really.

P. *coarctata*. Baby shrub with grey foliage. Tiny white scented flowers and shiny white berries. Good soil. Sunny spot. May. 3 in.

POLEMONIUM. A plant called Jacob's Ladder. Hardy, dainty. Grows anywhere but prefers semi-shade.

P. *carneum*. Flesh-pink flowers, pretty leaves. Summer. 9 in.

POLYGALA. Milkwort. The plants grown in the rock garden vary so much that they are best described separately.

P. chamaebuxus. Little bush with stiff, shiny leaves. Gorse-like flowers of white and yellow in May. 9 in. Loam soil, and either sun or shade.

P.c. purpurea. Like the above. Flowers pink and yellow.

P. vayredae. Narrow leaves. Flowers smaller, but stronger colour, being wine purple. 6 in.

POLYGONATUM. One of the Solomons Seal group. Loves peat and shade.

P. falcatum. Not unlike a Lily-of-the-Valley with pink flowers. June. 4-6 in.

P. hookeri. Rosy-lilac flowers on shortish stalks. Scree or alpine house. May. 2-3 in.

POLYGONUM. Knotweed. Useful plants for covering banks or walls in almost any soil or situation. Just watch that they do not over-run their neighbours. Increase by division.

P. affine. From a carpet of rather untidy leaves, spikes of pink flowers appear in June and continue until late autumn. 9 in.

P.a. 'Darjeeling Red'. Vigorous vivid crimson spikes. Summer. 9 in.

p. tenuicaule. A Japanese plant with spikes of white flowers and deep green leaves. Plant in shade. Spring. 3-4 in.

P. vaccinifolium. A neater-growing plant. The flower spikes are 4 in. high. The leaves turn beautiful shades of yellow and red in autumn.

POTENTILLA. The majority of these are too large and straggly for the rock garden, and are best kept in the flower borders. Ordinary garden soil.

P. aurea. Prostrate tufts of glossy leaves with golden flowers. May-July. 2 in.

P.a. chrysocraspeda 'Aurantiaca'. Lovely plants, orange flowers. Summer. 2-3 in.

P. eriocarpa. Neat bright green hummocks. Plants with yellow flowers. Summer. 1-2 in.

P. nepalensis 'Miss Wilmott'. Bright cherry-red flowers all summer. 6-12 in.

P. nitida. Silvery mat of leaves. Large, rose pink flowers on 1-in. high stems in summer.

P. recta 'Warrenii'. Masses of yellow flowers throughout

the summer. May be in flower at Christmas. 12 in.

P. tabernaemontani 'Nana'. A tiny plant, dark green leaves. Golden-yellow blossoms most of the summer. 1-2 in.

P. tonguei. Flowers an unusual shade of apricot with a red centre, produced over a long season, starting in June. Will flower in sun or semi-shade. 6 in.

PRIMULA. A huge family, from which it is difficult to select a few of the most suitable. Their requirements vary greatly, but by excluding the 'Bog Primulas' it is possible to say that good loam, frequently containing lime, and sunny positions will get good results.

P. auricula. The less formal varieties are lovely for the rock garden, and patches of mixed seedlings make a great show in spring. Avoid the heavy feeding that is given to produce show blooms, as the result would look out of place.

P.a. 'Blue Velvet'. A lovely plant. 6-8 in.

P.a. 'Byatt's Strain'. A fine range of colours. Spring. 6 in.

P.a. 'Decora'. Good deep blue. 6-8 in.

P.a. 'Old Yellow Dusty Miller'. Yellow flowers. Leaves covered with white farina. 6 in.

P.a. 'Old Red Dusty Miller'. Red. 6-8 in.

P. frondosa. Loves a moist well-drained soil. Neat rosettes, masses of dainty pink flowers. Semi-shade. May-June. 3 in.

P. integrifolia. Tubular rosy-lilac bell-shaped flowers. Early summer.

P. juliae. A creeping Primrose that needs good, rich soil. Does well in shade or sun. Many named hybrids like Pam, Bunty, Kinlough Beauty. All flower in the early spring. 2-4 in. Increase by division after flowering when leaf growth is at its most vigorous.

P. marginata. A lovely plant with serrated leaves covered with white mealy-looking substance. Clear lavender flowers in April. Parent of many beautiful hybrids such as Linda Pope and Marven.

P.x. pubescens. Not unlike an Auricula. The parent of a large race of garden hybrids, many of them good reds and rich purples. Popular examples are: The General, Mrs. Wilson, Red Star, Faldonside. Seed collected from these give plants of interest and variety.

P.x. 'Freedom'. Deep lilac flowers. 3-4 in.

P.x. 'The General'. Unusual, because a terra-cotta. 5 in.

P. rosea 'Grandiflora'. Lovely glowing carmine flowers. April-June. 6-9 in.

PULMONARIA. Lungwort. Useful plants for positions in sun or semi-shade and any ordinary garden soil. Increased by division.

P. angustifolia azurea. The best, with bright blue flowers in March and April. 8 in.

P. saccharata. Leaves have large white spots on them. Flowers shaded pink and blue.

PULSATILLA. 'Pasque Flower'.

P. vernalis. White flowers, flushed blue. Grows in bracts of silky-brown fur. Very charming. Gritty soil in the sun. 4 in.

P. vulgaris. Purple-violet flowers with golden stamens. Grows in the sun in any soil. April-May. 12 in.

RAMONDA. Beautiful plants needing a lime-free soil and a position facing north, but away from drips off trees. Increase by seed which is slow, or division of plants.

R. Nataliae. Rosettes of crinkled leaves. Flowers deep lavender with golden eye. May and June. 6 in.

R. pyrenaica. Dark-green rosettes. Erect stems bearing open flowers of clear lilac. 6 in. Does very well in pots in the alpine house.

RANUNCULUS. Buttercup. Only those introduced from alpine habitats will be mentioned.

R. glacialis. Grows in screes high up in the Alps. White flowers. 6 in.

R. montanus. 'Molten Gold'. Yellow flowers in a mass in spring and summer. Moist soil, sun. 4-6 in.

R. pyrenaeus. Cool, rich soil. White flowers with golden stamens in early summer. 6 in.

RAOULIA. Dwarf carpeters of exceptionally neat growth. Well-drained, sandy soil in full sun is needed for them to be seen at their best. Increased by division.

R. australis. Foliage quite silver. Flowers inconspicuous. Cannot tolerate winter damp.

R. glabra. Same type of growth as the above, but with green leaves.

R. tenuicaulis. Grey-green prostrate. Miniature yellow flowers. Spring. $\frac{1}{2}$ in.

ROSA. The miniature roses look attractive in the rock

garden. For soil they need good rich loam, as they are as
greedy as their full-sized brothers. Cuttings taken with a
heel will root in late summer.

R. *'Baby Gold'*. Gold and orange.

R. *'Dwarf King'*. Deep red.

R. *'Eleanor'*. Coral pink.

R. *'Margo Koster'*. Orange pink.

R. *'Oakington Ruby'*. Popular crimson.

R. *'Perle de Monserrat'*. Salmon pink.

R. *'Rouletti'*. Dainty pink.

R. *'Sweet Fairy'*. Silvery pink.

R. *'Yellow Doll'*. Pure yellow.

SANGUINARIA. One of the Poppy family called 'Blood-root'.

> *S. canadensis 'Flore Pleno'*. Blue-grey leaves with double
> snow-white flowers. Peaty soil. This plant does not
> 'stay' very long each year and is rare in consequence.
> April. 6 in.

SAPONARIA. Soapwort. An excellent plant for rock walls
where it can be allowed to make large cushions. Light,
well-drained soil in full sun. Easily raised from seed.

> *S. ocymoides*. Masses of trailing stems. Covered with
> rose-pink flowers in early summer. 6 in.

SAXIFRAGA. No general instructions can be given for
this family, as it comprises too many different types. They
are divided into groups, and each requires slightly different
treatment.

The Encrusted section (Euaizoonias) include those with
rosettes of tough leaves that are encrusted with white along
the margins. These require open situations in very gritty
soil, and do well in the upright crevices of large rocks. The
flowers are generally arching sprays of white, or pale pinks
and yellows.

> *S. burnattii.* A reddish-stemmed plant bearing glistening
> white flowers. 4 in.
>
> *S.b. 'Cecil Davis'*. The rosettes are silvery and the flower
> white. 6 in.
>
> *S. colchearis major*. Large rosettes, attractive.
>
> *S.c. minor*. Small rosettes – white flowers.
>
> *S. cotyledon pyramidalis*. Large-leaved rosette. Tall
> spines of pure white. 20 in.
>
> *S.c. 'Southside Seedling'*. Similar to above but with lovely

sprays of white blossoms spotted with crimson. May. 14 in.

Saxifraga 'South-side Seedling'

S. *pariculate baldensis*. Little green hummocks – white flowers. 2 in.

S.p. lutea. Similar to above with pale yellow blooms. 6 in.

S.p. rosea. A beautiful Bulgarian plant – deep pink. 6 in.

The mossy section (Dactyloides) requires a leafy loam, and must have a certain amount of moisture during the summer. Similar treatment suits the Umbrosa types, which are the London Pride saxifrages.

S. *decipiens*. Very many named hybrids from pure white, through pink, to deepest red. Flowering in May and June, heights vary from 4-9 in.

S. *hypnoides* 'Densa'. Tiny plant, moss-like, white flowers. Foliage turns crimson. 4 in.

S.h. 'Knapton Pink'. A beautiful pink. 9 in.

S.h. 'Mrs. Piper'. Deep pink touched with salmon. 9 in.

S.h. 'Peter Pan'. Very pretty. Compact, rich crimson. 3-4 in.

S.h. 'Wargrave'. A rich pink. 6 in.

S. *primuloides Elliot's var*. A smaller-growing plant. The flowers are a deep pink and they are only 6 in. high.

The Kabschia or Engleria section are dwarf, cushion-forming plants. They need well-drained, gritty soil and a sunny position. They are the earliest of the saxifrages to flower in the spring, and have a large range of colours. The named hybrids are very numerous, and in many cases hard to distinguish one from the other. They are perfect plants for crevices in bare rock, and in this position avoid getting over-run with moss – which is one of the most difficult 'weeds' to remove, as it gets right through the whole cushion of leaves.

S. apiculata. Easily grown. Deep-green leaves. Yellow. March. 3 in.

S.a. alba. White-flowered form of the above.

S. burseriana and its hybrids. Flowering from early in January, these are grand little plants with very large blooms on 2-in. stems.

S.b. crenata. White with the edges of the petals frilled.

S.b. sulphurea. Flowers soft sulphur-yellow.

S. elizabethae. Dark green, spiny leaves. Flowers strong yellow. Easy to grow and forms large clumps in a few seasons.

S. haagii. Bright-green cushions. Deep-yellow flowers with red buds. March-April. 2 in.

S. jenkinsii. One of the easiest of the close-growing types. Pale pink flowers on 1-in. stems cover the whole plant.

S. myra. Flat cushions of green. Deep pink flowers on very short stems in March. Very good in the scree.

S. kellereri. A beautiful plant with strong, silver green rosettes. Flowers are branching heads of pink very early in January. 3 in.

Another small section called Porphyrions. These are prostrate, trailing plants that need a gritty, peat soil, and a position where they will not get too dry in summer.

S. oppositifolia. The flowers are red-purple and practically stemless. Late February. 1 in.

S.o. splendens. Flowers larger than the above.

S. retusa. A miniature of the group. The flowers, which are tiny stars, are carried on branching stems 1 in. high.

The Engleria section are mid-way in appearance between the Kabschias and the Encrusteds, having flat rosettes of leaves that are broader than most of the Kabschias. Gritty soil and positions in full sun. The flowers are borne on stems a few inches high, generally curled over at the top. These stems are frequently covered with coloured hairs, which add to the general beauty of the plant.

S. *biasoletti*. Silver rosette of leaves. The arched flower spikes are red.

S. *grisebachii*. The most handsome of the section. Large rosettes of green leaves marked with silver. The flower spikes are 4 in. high, with reddish hairs, the petals pink and white. A large pan of this in the alpine house is a sight worth remembering.

There are other types that are not often used in the rock garden, so will not be mentioned in this book.

SCABIOSA. Need well-drained soil in a sunny position. Can be increased by seed or division of plants.

S. *graminifolia*. Long, narrow, greyish leaves. Large, lavender flowers on wiry stems all through the summer. 9 in.

S. *pterocephala* (syn. *parnassii*). Prostrate hummock of rounded, grey leaves. Covered with pinkish lilac flowers on 1-in. stems. Looks well in paving or on a rocky bank.

SCUTELLARIA. Skullcap. Compact little plant for a sunny position on a rock wall. Light soil is needed where it will spread by underground shoots. Increase by division or cuttings.

S. *alpina*. Purple and cream flowers. August. 6 in.

S. *hastata*. Short erect spikes of shimmering purple and lilac. Summer. 6 in.

S. *indica japonica*. Mauve pretty flowers, hairy leaves. Summer. 4 in.

SEDUM. Stonecrop. A large family of which only a collector would need more than a few. The naming is rather muddled as many of the species are very similar. They all have fleshy leaves and thrive in dry, sunny positions and light, sandy soil, though most of them will grow in any ordinary garden soil. Increase is no problem as the smallest bit will root in sand, and some varieties are too prolific with seed. They are invaluable for paving and walls, the varied colour of the leaves giving interest all the year round, as well as the large flower heads during the summer.

S. acre majus. A native stonecrop. Green leaves and golden flowers. 3 in.

S. album. Coral carpet. Another quick-growing plant. Bronzy-red flowers. 3 in.

S. anacampseros. Trailing stems 6 in. long, ending in heads of purple flowers in July.

S. dasyphyllum. Mauvish grey leaves. White flowers. 1 in.

S. anglicum. A carpeter, green leaves turning red in summer, white flowers. 1 in.

S. cauticola. Grey-green leaves. Rich rose-red flowers. August-September. 6 in.

S. divergens. Bronzy-red leaves. Yellow flowers. 2 in.

S. forsteranum. Leaves glaucous. Crimson-tipped yellow flowers. 4 in.

S.g. aureum. Golden leaves, pink flowers. 2 in.

S. hispanicum. Glaucous foliage. White flowers. 2 in.

S.h. 'Aureum'. Yellow foliage. Golden flowers.

S. kamtschaticum ellacombianum. Upright growth. Heads of deep gold flowers. 6 in.

S.k. middendorffanum. Upright growth. Golden flowers. 6 in.

S. lydium. The small green leaves go red at the tips in poor soil and look doubly attractive. Flowers white. 3 in.

S. populifolium. A little tree sedum that loses its leaves in winter. Flowers white. 9 in.

S. ruprestre 'Minus'. Bronzy-red leaves. Yellow flowers. 3 in.

S. sieboldii. Prostrate stems of grey leaves. Lovely pink flowers in August. 6 in.

S. spathulifolium. Rather large leaves covered with a grey 'bloom' like a ripe plum. Yellow flowers. 2 in.

S.s. purpureum. The leaves are a rich red, otherwise like the above. Both excellent for paving, screes or the alpine house.

S. spurium. Very rampant and thrives even in semi-shade. Pale pink, starry flowers. 6 in.

S.s. coccineus. The leaves have a reddish tinge. Flowers deep crimson. 6 in.

SEMPERVIVUM. Houseleek. Another huge family of plants with fleshy leaves, and again with great confusion as to naming. They form large, round, fleshy rosettes of

Sempervivums and Silver Saxifrages

various shades. The flower spikes are generally large. After flowering the rosette dies, but a ring of tiny offsets on runners carries on the life of the plant. They will grow almost anywhere – on the top of a bare wall with practically no soil, in a rock crevice or in paving; in fact, any place where the drainage is good. Waterlogged soil is about the only thing that will kill them. Increased by division of the offsets or by seed.

S. arachnoideum. The Cobweb Houseleek. Small rosettes covered with a mass of fine hairs like spiders' webs. The plant should have a pane of glass over it in winter to protect it from rain. Cold does not injure it. The flowers are large sprays of rosy pink. 6 in.

S.a. 'Stansfieldii'. A fine form. Its large rosettes turn red in late spring.

S. calcareum. Large rosettes of reddish purple with a grey sheen. Looks very well planted with other species of different colours.

S. giuseppii. Hairy, compact green rosettes.

S. glaucum. Bright green rosettes.

S. montanum. Dark green rosettes.

S.m. burnatii. Light green rosettes.

S. ornatum. Very handsome rosettes of deep ruby red.

S. tectorum calcareum 'Monstrosum'. Grey-green purple-tipped rosettes. Unusual.

S.t. 'Nigrum'. Rosettes apple-green. Red-tipped leaves.

S. soboliferum. Hen and Chicken's Houseleek. Small,

round rosettes of red and green. The offsets are produced in large numbers, like tiny marbles that sit on top of the old plants. Later these roll off and start a new colony farther down the slope.

SHORTIA. A woodland plant from Japan that needs a peat soil and a position in shade. Not easy to grow.

> *S. uniflora.* Leathery leaves. Large bell-shaped flowers, soft rose-pink in spring. 6 in.

SILENE. Catchfly. They need light soil in a sunny position and are easily increased from seed or cutting.

> *S. acaulis.* Neat cushions of glossy green leaves. Studded in summer with stemless, pink flowers. Very useful for providing green in the scree, as it tends to look very barren and stony in winter. 2 in.
>
> *S.a. 'Alba'.* A pretty white form.
>
> *S. alpestris.* White, starry flowers in May and June. 3 in.
>
> *S. schafta.* Large tufts of flower stems that produce many rosy magenta flowers in summer and for several months. 6 in. Excellent in the rock wall.

SISYRINCHIUM. Blue-eyed Grass. These look like miniature Irises, and have grassy leaves and starry flowers on the top of stiff stems. The petals close up at night. They grow in light soil in a sunny position and are easily increased by division.

> *S. angustifolium.* Clear blue flowers with a deeper eye. Summer. 4 in.
>
> *S. brachypus.* Dainty mass of pale yellow stars. Summer. 6 in.
>
> *S. bermudianum.* Violet blue flowers. 9 in.
>
> *S. californicum.* Bright yellow flowers. 9 in. Sets seed freely.

SOLDANELLA. Beautiful plants needing a damp soil of peat and coarse gravel. The flowers are hanging bells with fringed edges. Slugs are very fond of the flower buds, and will eat out the whole heart of the plant in the winter. Seed grows freely, but the tiny seedlings are awkward to handle, having very long, hairy roots making pricking out a fiddly job. Looks well grown in pans.

> *S. alpina.* Round, leathery leaves. Violet blue. 3 in. March and April.
>
> *S. montana villosa.* Like the above, but larger. 6 in.

SOLIDAGO. Golden Rod. Only one dwarf variety will be mentioned. Grows in any good garden soil, and is a suitable companion for the dwarf Michaelmas daisies. (Aster pygmaeus).

S. brachystachys. Bright yellow flowers. Autumn. 8 in. Tom Thumb is an interesting variety.

STACHYS. Often called 'Woundwort'. Prefers light soil and much sun.

S. discolor. White flowers, dark green foliage. June-August. 3 in.

S. lavandulifolia. Rosy-purple flowers and grey foliage. July-August. 6 in.

STATICE. Sea Lavender. Will grow in any well-drained garden soil. The 'everlasting' flowers are useful, flowering in August and remaining in good condition until the winter. Increase by seed.

S. bellidifolia. Small rosettes of tough, oval leaves. Sprays of mauve flowers. 6 in.

S. incana. Large sprays of white flowers with pinkish-mauve bracts and stems. 9 in.

STOKESIA. Often called the 'Stokes' Aster'. Loves the sun and good loam.

S. laevis 'Blue Star'. Lavender blue cornflower-like flowers. Late summer. 9 in.

TRADESCANTIA. A hardy perennial that does well anywhere, in sun or shade. Commonly called 'Spiderwort'.

T. brevicaulis. Bears brilliant rosy-crimson flowers on grassy foliage. 9-12 in.

THYMUS. Thyme. A useful family of fragrant herbs, the creeping varieties being the perfect plants to clothe paving, as they do not resent a reasonable amount of traffic, and also give out their spicy smell when crushed underfoot. Light soil in full sun is needed. Most varieties are easily increased by division.

T. citriodorus Silver Queen. Lemon-scented bush of variegated leaves. Flowers pale mauve in July. 9 in.

T. Doone Valley. New, mat-forming. Gold and bright green leaves – lovely.

T. herba-barona. The Caraway scented thyme. Spreading growth and deep purple flowers. June. 4 in.

T. serpyllum. A creeping variety for covering walls and paving. There are many forms of different colours. They start flowering in June and continue to give a display of colour until August. 1 in.

T.s. Annie Hall. Green leaves. Flowers flesh pink.

T.s. carneus. Dark green leaves. Pink flowers.

T.s. coccineus. Deep reddish-green leaves. Flowers crimson.

T.s. minus. Pink flowers. A carpeter. ½ in.

T.s. Pink Chintz. A salmon pink.

T.s. Snowdrift. A lovely white.

T.s. major. Leaves larger than the others. Flowers crimson. 2 in.

THALICTRUM. A beautiful Maidenhair-like plant, loves peaty soil, grows in sun or shade.

T. kiusianum. Flowers feathering, of a rosy lavender colour. 3 in.

TROLLIUS. The globe flower – a member of the buttercup family. Likes a moist spot.

T. acaulis. Open yellow cups. May-June. 3 in.

T. pumilus. Orange-yellow saucers. Summer. 9 in.

TUNICA. Useful for seeding about among other plants, but should not be planted by itself, as the whole plant is too light and feathery to cover the ground. Any ordinary garden soil in a sunny position.

T. saxifraga. Rosette. Double pale pink flowers on wiry stems from June till September. Looks like Gypsophila. 6 in.

T.s. 'Alba Plena'. Looks like a baby double white Gypsophila.

VERBENA. This plant is not hardy, but is included because it supplies a colour that is very scarce in the rock garden. Will spread quickly, rooting as it goes, in light soil in a sunny position. Cuttings root easily, and a few kept in a frame or house for winter will ensure a supply for the next year. Watch out for greenfly, which are often troublesome on the young shoots.

V. chamaedryfolia (syn. *peruviana*). Prostrate growth. Large, round flower heads of intense scarlet all through the summer.

V. tenera 'Mahonettii'. Violet red flowers striped white. Summer. 3 in.

VERONICA. Speedwell. A huge family of plants that includes shrubs, tall herbaceous plants and low-spreading plants. Most of them will grow in ordinary garden soil and prefer sunny positions. Can be increased by cuttings, division and seed.

V. bidwilli minor. Tiny little leaves on thread-like stems.

Grow for the foliage, and the small, white flowers will not be a disappointment. 2 in. Does well in the scree or alpine house.

V. cinerea. Silver leaves. Spikes of blue flowers. 4 in.

V. corallii. Spikes of deep salmon pink. Very pretty. July-August. 9 in.

V. incana. Grey leaves. Spikes of deep blue flowers in July. 9 in.

V. pectinata. Prostrate woolly leaves. Sprays of blue flowers in May and June.

V.p. rosea. Like the above with pink flowers.

V. repens. Shiny, green leaves that lie close to the ground, the stems rooting as they go. White flowers in May. 1 in.

V. selleri 'Shirley Blue'. Brilliant gentian-blue spikes, rather tall however. June-July. 1 ft.

V. spicata. Rather like V. incana, but with green leaves. There are pink, blue and white flowered forms.

V. telephifolia. Creeping mats of glaucous foliage with pale blue flowers. July-August. 2 in.

V. teucrium dubia, or *V. prostrata* or *V. rupestris* – they all seem to be the same plant. An excellent plant, easy to grow, that covers the ground with a mat of green leaves. Covered with 3-in. long 'tails' of bright blue flowers in May. Rosea is a pink form and Nana a deep blue type.

V.t.d. 'Waterperry Blue'. A lovely bright blue. 1 in.

V. whitleyi. Deep blue creeping variety. 2-3 in.

VIOLA. These plants need good soil to do well and give a good show of flowers. Increased in various ways, according to variety.

V. cornuta minor. Easily grown. Produces masses of slender, butterfly flowers in spring and summer. Flowers are white, shades of light blue and good purple.

V. cucullata albiflora. Similar to large white Violets. Summer. 4-6 in.

V. labradorica 'Purpurea'. Like small Violets with purplish leaves. Summer. 2-3 in.

V. rupestris 'Rosea'. Like a pink Violet. Summer. 3 in.

ZAUSCHNERIA. Californian Fuchsia. A grand plant for giving a display of orange in the autumn garden. Spreads freely by underground stems, if planted in good, light loam in a sunny position. Once settled, it will penetrate into narrow cracks in the rocks and thrive on very little soil. Increase by division. This is best done after growth has started in spring.

Z. californica. Spikes of tubular orange flowers in August and September. 12 in.

Z. cana. Greyish leaves, orange-scarlet trumpetlike flowers. Summer. 12 in.

A water garden, with lilies in the foreground

Throughout the ages people have felt the need of water in their gardens. The Monasteries had their fish ponds so that the monks could easily collect their fish for Fridays. The Indian and Persian gardener found water necessary for irrigation, and perhaps it really is to the East that we owe much of our love of pools – for cool places are certainly appreciated by those who live in the warmer climes. There is a Persian motto referring to a pool which says 'If there is a Heaven upon earth – it is here – it is here.'

The pool may be of value for the reflections it gives, and even in quite a small garden reflections can be arranged. There is always the biological reflection, the fish and the other water life, apart from the beauty and scent of Aquatic Plants.

The pool can either be formal or informal. The formal pool could be a centre piece and form a special 'garden' on its own. It is often placed at the bottom of the lawn, or even quite near the house, as an adjunct to a paved pathway or court. If informal, it can be made close to the rock garden and will then be connected to it by a small stream. It may be situated in a particular part of the

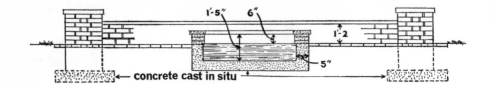

garden because of a natural depression there, and may be excavated in such a manner that it looks natural. Each garden presents its own problems, but somewhere in most gardens there is room and possibly a need, for a small or even a large water garden.

A formal garden pool: (above) cross-section, and (below) plan view

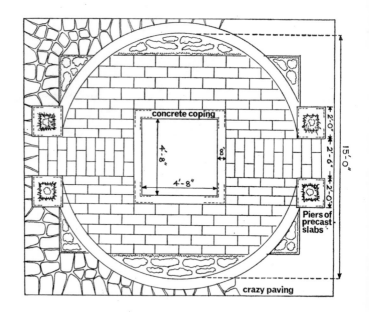

The round dish-shaped' pool

The most simple pool to make is the 'dish-shaped' pool, which does not require any shuttering.

Excavate the ground, making the sides to a flat slope. In selecting the site, choose one that is on undisturbed soil and away from any trees, otherwise there is a likelihood of the pond cracking.

After the soil has been dug, it should be well rammed, and any soft places filled in with clinker or rubble to get a firm, even sub-base. This is essential: the 'dish' rests on the earth, and if one part of the ground is much softer

Five steps in the construction of a small dish-shaped pool lined with P.V.C. (see p. 123)

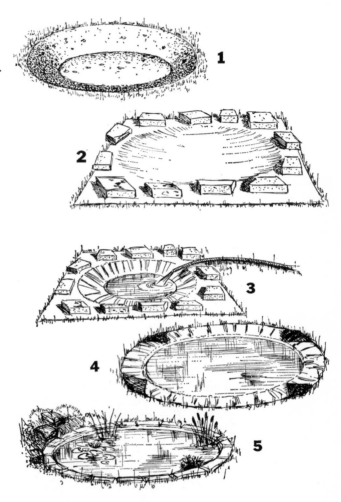

than another, the 'dish' will tend to sink in the soft places, which may lead to cracks appearing.

When preparation of the ground has been completed, use a concrete composed of one part of cement and three parts of sand to line the surface. Its thickness should be at least 3 in. Additional strength can be obtained if stout wire netting is placed in the centre of the concrete to act as reinforcement.

Another good tip is to cover the soil with a stout polythene sheet before placing the concrete. This will help to prevent the soil from absorbing water from the concrete.

The pond can be made to any shape by this method, but its size should not exceed about 4 ft. in diameter, and the depth should not be greater than 18 in., otherwise difficulty will arise in placing the concrete in one operation.

A very delightful effect can be obtained with sloping ground and a series of small pools. Another idea is to dig a circular channel to form an island in the centre.

The rectangular pool

A very simple type of pool is one which is rectangular. The great advantage of this type of pool is that a varying depth of water can be provided, one end being 12 in. or so deeper than the other. It is usual also to provide a ledge about 12 in. wide and 4 in. below the normal water level so that if fish are kept, the 'fry' will find a hiding place during the spawning season where they will not be worried by other fish. Alternatively, the bottom of the pool can be stepped so as to provide a shallow area.

Sectional view of a rectangular pool

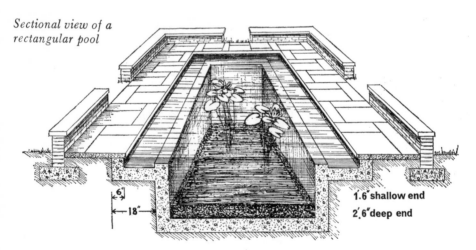

6"
18"
1.6" shallow end
2'.6" deep end

The thickness of the concrete depends on the depth of water, but a thickness of at least 4 in. will be required for most ponds.

A typical design for a lily pond will be found in the illustration above. It will be seen that the greatest depth is 2 ft. 6 in. at one end, and that the bottom is sloped up to a depth of 1 ft. 6 in. at the other end. The length and width will depend on the size of the garden.

Site preparation

When the position of the pool and the design have been decided upon, it is necessary to carry out soil excavation. The topsoil should first be removed and the position of the pool marked out with pegs and string lines. Disposal of the excavated soil should not present a problem, as it can be used for making a raised bed around the pool to give it a sunken effect.

After digging is completed, the bottom of the pool should be well rammed and levelled to provide a firm and even base for the concrete. In cases where the ground is soft, a 3-in. layer of broken bricks, rubble or similar dry material should be spread over the bottom and well rammed. This will tighten the soil and help to make a firm base.

Construction of the pool

The next step is concreting the bottom of the pool. Whether it can be accomplished in one operation will depend largely on the size of the pool and the facilities available for mixing the concrete. Timber pegs should be driven in at intervals across the width and along the length of the pool, the tops of which should be level with the desired thickness of concrete.

An easy method for setting these pegs is to fix one at each end of the pool at the correct level, and then by means of a tightened string attached to the end pegs, to drive the other pegs in at suitable intervals until their tops are level with the string.

Mixing the concrete   The materials required for concrete-making are cement, sand, and shingle. For pool work the concrete should be composed of one part of cement, two parts of sand, and three parts of shingle, graded from ¾-in. down to 3/16ths in. In some localities it may be found necessary to use crushed stone for the aggregate instead of shingle. This is quite satisfactory, provided the material does not contain any very fine dust. The cement, sand, and shingle should all be measured by volume in the same size receptacle, so as to obtain the correct proportions.   An ordinary bucket is quite suitable for this purpose.

After the cement and sand have been thoroughly mixed in their dry state the shingle or broken stone is added, and the whole mix is then given a further turning before the water is added. The water should be added a little at a time while the materials are being turned over until a plastic and easily workable mix is obtained.

Placing the concrete   Immediately before placing the concrete, the bottom of the excavation should be covered with polythene sheeting. The concrete is then spread over the polythene, using a stout piece of timber for tamping, until it is level with the top of the pegs. These pegs should be removed as the work progresses, and the top surface should be finished off with a wooden float.

The edges of the floor slab on which the walls will rest should be roughened in order to form a key between the sides and the bottom. This is important, as pools sometimes leak at this junction due to an imperfect joint.

Where it is not possible to complete the slab in a day, a straight piece of wood should be placed across the width of the pool and the concrete finished at this point. To complete the slab, the timber is removed and the edge of the slab roughened. The loose pieces of concrete should be removed, and immediately before placing the new concrete, the roughened edge should be given a thick coat of cement grout, made by mixing equal parts of cement and sand with water to the consistency of thick oil paint.

After the slab has hardened sufficiently, it should be covered with polythene to prevent the concrete from drying out too quickly.

Placing concrete in frosty weather   It should be noted that concrete work should not be carried out when the temperature is below 35 degrees F. on a falling thermometer, but during mild weather conditions when the day temperatures are above 35 degrees F. and the night temperatures a few degrees below freezing point, concrete work may be carried out by using hot water for mixing. The temperature of the water should be about 150 degrees F. Mixing is carried out in the usual manner, the cement, sand and stone being mixed first in their dry state before the water is added.

On no account should the hot water be added to the cement alone. Frozen aggregate should be thawed by pouring a few buckets of water (boiling) over the heap.

When water of the above temperature is added to the mix, the temperature of the concrete is raised about 65 degrees F., i.e., summer temperature, thus providing sufficient heat for the chemical action involved in the. setting and hardening of the cement to take place.

In order that the heat may be retained and the chemical action continued, all newly placed concrete should be covered at night with polythene sheeting, straw, sacks, hessian or similar dry material which should be firmly held down in order to prevent it from becoming dislodged. Sacks partly filled with straw and laid flat on the surface give excellent protection.

The protective covering should be kept in position until the concrete has hardened.

Although the concrete made in winter is slow in hardening, the desired result is eventually obtained, and no anxiety need be felt if the concrete remains soft for one or two days.

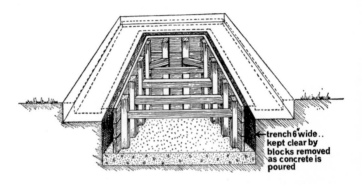

The shuttering used in pool construction

trench 6″ wide .. kept clear by blocks removed as concrete is poured

Shuttering The timber framework for the walls of a rectangular pool does not call for a very great knowledge of carpentry, and can quite easily be constructed by the amateur. The framework generally consists of a bottomless box, securely battened and braced to prevent the timber from bulging during the placing of the concrete.

The drawing above shows the form for a pool, consisting of 1-in. boards battened together with 2-in. by 2-in. timbers, and securely braced so that it will be rigid. The formwork is made in panels, and erected in the pool. To prevent it from moving, the forms should be blocked on all sides against the earth. This is shown in the drawing, the blocks being removed as the wall concrete is placed.

In order to facilitate the removal of the forms, it is

advisable to oil the surface against which the concrete will be placed. Proprietary brands of mould oil, specially made for the purpose, can be obtained.

Concreting the sides   The mix of concrete given for the floor is also recommended for the walls. Concrete should be placed in even layers, working gradually round the pool, and consolidated with a stout piece of timber.

If the walls cannot be completed in a day, then it will be necessary to form a horizontal construction joint. The concrete at this joint should be left fairly level and protected from the weather by covering the wall at the top of the formwork with polythene sheet or sacking.

Before proceeding with the concreting, roughen the surface, taking care to remove any loose pieces of concrete, and apply a thick coat of cement grout so that new concrete will form a proper bond with that already placed.

Removing the shuttering   The forms should be left in position for at least three days. After the timbers have been removed the pond may be filled with water, and the water level marked on the side in pencil.

During the first few days, it is usual to find a considerable drop in the water-level. This does not mean that the pool leaks, as a certain amount of water is absorbed by the concrete. Losses due to evaporation, which are quite considerable on a very hot day, also have to be considered.

The round, flat-bottomed pool

This is made in the same way as the rectangular pool, but the formwork may consist of a circular framework of timber to which is secured plywood or some other material which is easily bent to shape.

Seasoning

Before plants or fish are introduced, it is necessary to season the pool. The usual method is to fill the pool and leave it for a week or so, and after this period to scrub the sides vigorously with a hard brush. The pond should then be emptied and refilled. This process should be carried out two or three times before the pond is ready for stocking.

Another method, which has proved quite successful, is to paint the inside of the pool with a 1-in-4 solution of waterglass. This needs to be done two or three times at intervals of two or three days.

Whichever method is adopted, great care should be taken

to see that the seasoning is perfect, and this can be done by introducing a few tadpoles or even small goldfish into the water. If they show no ill effects, then the pond is seasoned and safe to be stocked with more expensive fish.

Another method is to paint the inside of the pool with a bituminous paint. Fortunately these paints can be obtained in colours, and their use enables the owner to provide the pool with a coloured finish. Another great advantage of a bituminous paint is that it is waterproof, and so the impermeability of the pool is increased. The blue and green bituminous paints look very attractive.

Coping

The coping stones to be used around the edge of the pond can be made with concrete slabs of any shape and size. The great advantage of using coping stones of some kind is that they may be laid so that they project over the edge of the pool, and so hide any irregularities of the pool walls. It is easy to change the appearance of a rectangular pond to the shape of an informal pool if the slabs are laid irregularly around the edges.

The pool surround

It is sometimes necessary to lay paving stones as a surround to the pool, and these may be made at home with cement and sand. By making various sizes of slabs, very attractive patterns can be formed, as will be seen in the diagrams on page 122.

It is quite simple to lay the concrete *in situ* and before it has hardened to cut double lines into the surface, $\frac{3}{8}$ in. apart and about $\frac{1}{2}$ in. deep, to conform to the pattern it is desired to reproduce. These lines form the joint lines, and when the concrete has hardened, the concrete between these lines may be removed to give an appearance of paving.

Pool liners or 'ready-made' pools

In addition to making pools with concrete, it is possible to buy a wide range of pools of various sizes and shapes made of fibreglass or plastic. The gardener has to excavate the ground to fit the shape of the 'pool' he has bought and then place it firmly in position. The outside edges will then be hidden by the use of stones or rocks. Those who sell these ready-made pools will be glad to give full instructions as to their use.

In the case of pool liners, it is usual to use P.V.C. or

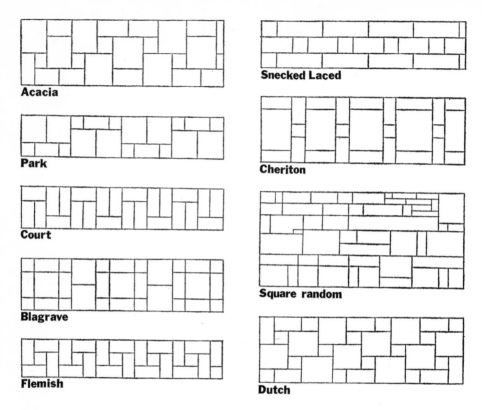

Acacia

Snecked Laced

Park

Cheriton

Court

Square random

Blagrave

Flemish

Dutch

Surrounds for a
pool

Butyl Rubber sheeting and to stick to a simple pool outline, i.e. one with no sharp angles or corners. The P.V.C. may be bought in a light blue shade but the Butyl Rubber is always black. Both are chemically inert and need no special treatment. The Butyl Rubber on the whole has a better stretch than P.V.C. and so is easier to use.

To work out the sheeting required, remember that the length of the sheet is the overall length of the pool plus twice its maximum depth. The width of the sheet will be again the overall width of the pool plus, again, twice its maximum depth. So a pool 10 ft. by 6 ft. by 24 in. needs a liner 14 ft. by 10 ft.

You can get ready-made liners manufactured from Terylene P.V.C. They are blue on one side and grey on the

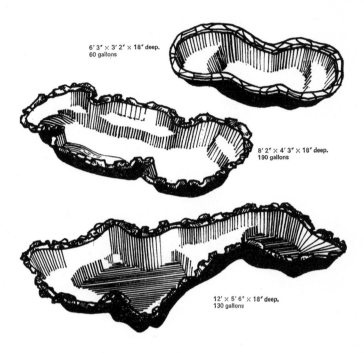

6' 3" × 3' 2" × 18" deep.
60 gallons

8' 2" × 4' 3" × 18" deep.
190 gallons

12' × 5' 6" × 18" deep.
130 gallons

Fibre glass pools

other. They are made from double-laminated P.V.C. with nylon mesh reinforcement. For a pool 5 ft. by 3 ft., order an 8ft. by 6 ft. sheet. For a pool 9 ft. by 5 ft., order a 12 ft. by 8 ft. sheet, while for a pool 15 ft. by 9 ft., order a sheet 18ft. by 12 ft.

Making a P.V.C. pool

Choose your ground preferably away from trees. Dig out the soil to the size and shape desired, firming the earth thoroughly afterwards. Be sure to remove rough stones and sharp objects. Sift soil or sand over the bottom of the shaped pool so as to provide the lining sheet with a smooth bed.

Lay down the P.V.C. evenly over the area concerned and stretch it fairly tightly. Now secure the edges of the liner with bricks or large stones so that as the water is poured in, it takes the liner down evenly. Fill in with water from a hose slowly and the material will stretch and lie in position. When the pool is full, leave it for a few days and then, with a sharp pair of shears, trim off any excess liner all round BUT leaving a 6-in. edge to form a flat surface. On this flat surface place paving slabs in a regular or ir-

regular pattern as desired. If the paving stones overhang
the pool edge by 2 in., the best results are achieved both
for the sake of the plants and fish. (See drawing on p. 115.)

If your pool is to be a success and is not going to be 'smelly' or a breeding place for insects, it will be necessary for you to put in plants of various kinds. There is a very wide choice of plants, fortunately : floating Aquatics, Oxygenators, Ordinary Aquatics, Ferns, Rushes and tall-growing perennials for the surrounds. These, with the fish and the crustacea will help to keep the water sweet.

Controlling algae

Soon after the pool has been stocked with plants and fish, the clarity of the new water disappears. Many owners are distressed by this, and immediately consider emptying the pool and refilling. This should not be done, as clouding is part of a natural cycle. The water turns opaque, and subsequently becomes green. The opaqueness is due to chemical changes in the soil used either in the bottom of the pool or in the pots that are submerged, and the greenness is due to algae (microscopic plants).

Providing the pool has been properly stocked with the correct plants and livestock to give the necessary balance, the water should again become perfectly clear in a few months. Sometimes this takes as long as eighteen months.

Providing they do not get too numerous, algae do no harm to the fish, indeed they benefit them. Algae are great oxygenators. Where algae growth is excessive it will exhaust the water constituents upon which it is sustained, and so ultimately it will diminish to normal proportions. It is in the newly-built pond that the propagation of the algae is very rapid, and it is always greatest in a pool exposed to strong sunlight.

One kind of algae is known as Blanket Weed, and this may prove troublesome. It makes excessive and dense growth and may even strangle other aquatic plants and even harm small fishes. This weed is often introduced accidentally when planting aquatic plants which have been obtained from pools in the country. The long, hair-like green threads combine into a solid mat – hence the name 'blanket weed'.

If excessive growth of this weed does appear, it is necessary to remove all pond life and sterilize the pool with permanganate of potash. This is done by placing a handful of crystals in a muslin bag, attaching this to the end of a stick or piece of string, and then swirling it about in the water until it has changed to a rich purple colour. After a day's soaking, the pool may be emptied and replenished with fresh water, care of course, being taken to see that most of the solution is removed.

Another method of control is by the use of powdered copper sulphate, but very little copper sulphate is necessary. If the minutest quantities are used then the goldfish are not harmed. All that is required is an amount equal to $\frac{1}{8}$ oz. per 1,000 gallons. Such a dose may be applied at one-monthly intervals if necessary during the spring and autumn.

Other methods of helping to control the growth of algae are : (1) to plant marginal plants or bushes on the sunny side of the water so as to give shade; (2) to introduce water lilies or other floating aquatics; and (3) to stock the pond with various crustacea, such as water fleas, cyclops and aquatic snails.

Balance

The waste matter which accumulates in the pool is considerable, and this makes it essential that sufficient plants are grown to absorb all this material. As a general guide, I should say that one plant is necessary to every sq. ft., or at any rate, every 2 sq. ft., but this includes the smaller-growing subjects as well as the larger ones. The more sparsely the pool is planted, the longer it takes to mature.

It may be necessary to layer the pond with soil and to plant the various aquatics that need it in this. A heavy fibrous meadow loam is excellent for the purpose. It is always better to avoid sand, leaf-mould and peat or the soil from ponds or rivers. The loam should be spread on the bottom of the pool to the depth of 6 or 7 in. and it should be slightly moistened and then well rammed.

It is possible to furnish the pool with plants grown in pots, and these may either be stood on shelving, made specially for the purpose, or on temporary stands dropped into the pool.

Where water lilies are to be grown, place twelve-months-old, well-decayed cow manure in the bottom of the pool first of all, and then put the soil on top. Quite a good substitute is a coarse bonemeal, and a 1/16th oz. dusting all over the bottom of the pool should be sufficient.

There is a common belief that it is necessary to cover the soil with sand or shingle, and that this will help to keep the water clear. There is no need to do this, for the use of shingle has nothing to do with the clearness, which, as has already been stated, will be brought about if there is a correct balance of plants, fish and snails.

13 Water Lilies

To be successful with water lilies you must put them in the sun reaches them from midday until the late afternoon. Water lilies should be planted after the middle of April, anyway, and the plant soon grows out new roots directly and during the months of May and June, just after the plants have started growing vigorously.

The roots of many of the species are extremely retentive of life, and I have known them to be out of water for many months without losing vitality. The majority of water lilies open their flowers during the day and close them during the late afternoon, but some of the tropical forms wait until the cool of the evening before they bloom and start to scent the air. Some lilies hold themselves erect out of the water as if reaching upwards for the sun; most, however, float on the surface of the pool and gently move as the breezes disturb the shimmering smoothness of the water.

The plants are lifted by severing nearly all the roots. These should never be confused with the root stock or the hard, fleshy part. Old roots would never take fresh hold a full sunny position, or at any rate, in a position where it is transplanted. Some varieties have roots like bananas; others are like the base of celery; others are like small potatoes or even nuts. The banana-like roots should be planted horizontally, the root being covered with 1 in. of soil and the crown left just exposed. Those with celery-like roots should have a hole of sufficient size made for them, to enable the plant to be set upright with the shortened roots pointing downwards and the crown just exposed. Those with potato or nut-like roots may be planted in a similar manner to the first group.

In every case firm planting is necessary. Pressure should be applied around the root, but not so much pressure that the fragile parts are damaged.

The observant man will notice from the soil mark, or from the growth or shape, how the water lily has been previously planted, and he can then imitate this as nearly as possible.

In order to prevent the plant from rising at all while the water is running into the pool, large stones may be placed around it and these can be left in position for, say, six weeks. After this time the new roots should have developed.

Various other methods of planting have been devised :

(1) The planting of the water lily in a basket of compost, the crown being wedged into place by a series of turves cut to shape. These prevent the soil from escaping when the basket is lowered into position. (2) Instead of small baskets, shallow perforated aquatic pans may be used. These are specially made for the purpose and can be planted up in a similar manner to the baskets.

It is always best to cover the plants with only a few inches of water until growth commences, and then as the plants progress, the pool may be filled. Shallow water warms more quickly, and it is this warmth that encourages early growth.

Sometimes the plants have to be dropped into position after the pools have been filled, and in this case it is better to place the pans or baskets on to some temporary shelving made with bricks, and then as the plants progress, to lower them gradually.

Frost and the pool

In the spring, when the water lilies are just bursting into growth, all the rubbish and dead leaves which may have accumulated during the winter months can be cleared away. It is sometimes a good thing to drain the pool, and then remove 2 or 3 in. of mud for, say, 1 in. round the crown of the water lily and replace this with good fresh soil.

If the hardy species of water lilies are grown, they can withstand all the frost that we experience in this country. The pool should be kept filled during the winter so that there is at least 10 in. of water covering the crown.

It is advisable when the pool is frozen to break the ice from time to time, which helps to keep the fish supplied with air. Some people prefer to cover the pool, or part of the pool with boards or sacking, so as to prevent the water from freezing underneath.

For smaller pools there are proprietary pool heaters which are normally sufficient to keep a corner of the pool free from ice. One pool heater is sufficient for pools up to 25 sq. ft. in surface area, but two heaters are necessary in pools up to 60 sq. ft. in area.

A heater provided with 6 ft. of cable sealed off into the unit is sufficient to reach a point adjacent to the pool. Connection is made here, using a weatherproof cable connector, of the right length of correct cable so as to lead back to the nearest earthed source of mains electricity. The same wiring can also be used to produce a fountain in summer months.

Pests that attack water-lilies

MOSQUITO LARVAE. This pest appears early in summer, attacking both the leaves and the buds. The leaves turn yellow and the buds fail to mature. It is a very serious pest with young plants.

Control. Stock the pond with surface-eating fish, such as golden carp, rudd and gold or silver orfe.

BLACK FLY. These aphides attack the flowers and the leaves during dry, sunny weather. The plants look most unsightly and the sucking of the sap may mar the perfection of the blooms.

Control. Spray with water by means of a hose or a syringe and so wash the aphides into the pool, where they will be devoured by the fish.

In very bad cases, paraffin emulsion may be used, the formula being $\frac{1}{2}$ oz. of soft soap (or a substitute 'spreader'), and 1 quart of boiling water to which is added $\frac{1}{2}$ pint of paraffin. This should be well mixed together by constant stirring and beating (it is better to keep the mixture hot while stirring is going on), and then should be added to 5 gallons of cold water. The final mixture may be sprayed on to the plants. Fish seldom suffer any harmful effect from such spraying.

ACCENTROPUS NIVEUS. If a silvery white butterfly is seen fluttering over the pool during a summer evening, then an attack of the Accentropus may be feared. The larva of this butterfly cuts irregular, circular holes in the leaves of water lilies and then joins these together into a little 'cubby hole' where it may pupate.

Control. Stock the pool with fish as suggested for the mosquito larva.

A list of varieties of water lilies

There are many more varieties of Water Lilies than people realize. The types range from white and pinks, to reds, crimsons and yellows. Then there are the singles and doubles, the highly-scented kinds, and those with round, cup-like flowers or with star-shaped flowers.

For water over 3 ft. deep, only the most vigorous kinds can be grown, and these are the varieties that should be grown in baskets. They should be planted temporarily in shallow water before being finally plunged in their permanent home.

The varieties have been classified into four groups, according to the depth at which they are best planted, and the area of the water they cover :

(A) Plant in 6-12 in. of water. May cover an area of 24 in.

(B) Plant in 1 ft. of water. May cover an area of 4 ft.

(C) Plant in 2 ft. of water. May cover an area of 7 ft.

(D) Plant in 3 ft. of water. May cover an area of 10 ft.

Group A

LAYDECKERI

> *L. fulgens.* The medium flowers are bright carmine to amaranth. The foliage is olive green with brown red spots. Flowers very freely and is good for small pools. Sweet scent.

ODORATA

> *O. minor.* Small, star-shaped flowers of white with yellow anthers. The foliage is pale green and the leaves are small. Very fine scent and a good choice for a pool.

TETRAGONA

> *T. pygmaea helvosa.* Attractive olive green foliage, heavily mottled maroon. A profusion of small, star-shaped, rich sulphur yellow flowers.

> *T. pygmaea alba.* This is one of the smallest and daintiest of the water lilies. It has light green foliage, rounded, and tiny, star-shaped, snow white flowers.

Group B

ALBATROSS (syn. *ALBA*). Large star-shaped flowers, snow white, conspicuous golden yellow anthers; young foliage is dark purple changing to dark green.

CANDIDA. Free flowering lilies for the small pool. Vigorous and easily established.

SOLFATARE. A good grower suitable for the small pool. More orange than yellow with mottled leaves.

ELLISIANA. Medium sized flowers of vermilion red. The sepals are white, stained rose. Orange stamens. Olive green foliage.

FIRECREST. The flowers, medium size, are rich rose pink with brilliant orange stamens tipped fiery red, and are produced in great profusion.

FROEBELI. An old variety, scented. The flowers are medium, very rich wine-colour and the foliage dark green with large leaves.

ODORATA. White flowers, medium cup-shaped, scented. They open in early June and go on to October.

> *O. sulphurea (Odorata mexicana).* Dark olive green foliage, heavily mottled reddish brown. Soft sulphur yellow flowers.
>
> *O. turicensis.* Medium sized, free flowering, rose pink. Delicious scent.

RENE GERARD. Very attractive, large-sized rich rose-crimson flowers, freely produced. A well-recommended and easily-grown variety.

SIRIUS. Large, deep rosy-red blooms, with glowing red stamens. Handsome foliage.

SOMPTUOSA. Very large flower, rose pink spotted white. Inner petals deep rose, outer petals rose stained green. Deep orange stamens. Lovely scent.

Group C

AMABILIS. The large star-shaped flowers are salmon shaded white, to rose and deep pink in centre. The foliage is reddish, going green later.

BRAKLEYI.

> *B. rosea (Tuberosa odorata rosea).* Medium sized cup-shaped flowers are a glistening rose pink, standing well above the water. Delightful scent.

ESCARBOUCLE. Bright crimson flowers with matching stamens, and large. The foliage is green, The flowers are free and lasting. This variety could also be in Group B.

GONNERE. Large, double, snow white flowers, the outer petals stained and striped green. Yellow stamens. Free flowering and lasts a long time.

INDIANA. Flowers medium to large, yellowish orange changing through bronze orange to coppery red. Deep green foliage spotted maroon. A distinctive variety.

JAMES BRYDON. Pæony-shaped flower, crimson pink, with golden stamens. The young leaves are purple going green with age. Needs plenty of room.

MADAME WILFRON GONNERE. A very handsome lily, producing large bowl-shaped, double flowers of deep rose pink.

MARLIACEA.

>*M. carnea.* The flowers are blush white, stained rose towards the base of the petals. When transplanted, the flowers are usually pure white the first year. A strong growing variety with large flowers.
>
>*M. chromatella.* A creamy yellow with an orange centre. The floating leaves are marked wine red.
>
>*M. rosea.* Large flowers of glistening softest pink. Dark green foliage. Popular.
>
>*M. albida.* Handsome blooms, freely produced, white.

MASANIELLO. Very large, pæony-like flowers, carmine rose minutely spotted carmine. Deep yellow stamens. The flowers stand several inches out of the water.

Group D

ATTRACTION. Bright purplish crimson, slightly flaked white. Deep mahogany stamens. Very large flowers. The foliage is first green purple then olive green.

CHARLES DE MEURVILLE. An exceptionally free-flowering lily producing enormous wine-red blooms. For the large pool only.

COLONEL A. J. WELCH. Bright yellow, large, star-shaped flowers borne on stems 6 in. long. Very free flowering. Pale green foliage.

TUBEROSA.

>*Tuberosa alba gladstoniana.* Pure white pæony-like flowers. Green shading in the sepals. Needs so much room that it should only be grown in lakes and ponds.
>
>*T. maxima.* Very vigorous variety with shell-shaped petals. Snow white. Can be grown in 3-4 ft. of water. When planted in shallow water, the flowers stand 6-9 in. out of the water.
>
>*T.m. rosea.* Bright green foliage, flowers a soft pink shaded white. Fragrant.

VIRGINALIS. Very large flowers with shell-shaped petals, snow white and rose at base. Golden yellow stamens. Flowers from May till September.

14 Aquatic Plants

In addition to the water lilies, there are a large number of miscellaneous aquatics which can be grown in your pool. Some will be used to break straight lines and clothe the rough edges. Most will help to create more natural effects, and all will help in the build-up of the pool as described in Chapter 12. Some will be grown in a more central position of the pool and some will be grown close to the margin. Care must be taken with the plants that have a creeping habit, as if these are not kept under control, they may well smother other specimens. If it is necessary to put in plants of this kind, see that the roots are constricted in a concrete box or pan, or that they are planted in a kind of pocket out of which they cannot escape.

Ordinary aquatics may be planted in very much the same way as the water lily and in similar heavy, fibrous loam. The loam should be moistened before being introduced into the pool, and when in position, should be pressed down firmly. The chosen aquatics are then planted in the moist soil, and the pool filled with water.

Some plants need their crowns covered with 4 or 5 in. of water, others with 12 or 15 in., and some even with only 2 or 3 in. Some plants have their flowers and foliage floating above the surface, some have their foliage and flowers standing well above the water level. I have therefore deemed it necessary to divide the varieties up into seven groups :

1. Crown covered with 3-5 in. of water, foliage under water, flowers floating on or above water.
2. Crown covered with 3-5 in. of water, foliage above water, flowers above water.
3. Crown covered with 12-15 in. of water, foliage floating on surface, and flowers floating on surface.
4. Crown covered with 3-5 in. of water, foliage floating on surface, and flowers floating on surface.
5. Crown covered with 2-4 in. of water.
6. Crown covered with 12-15 in. of water, foliage well above water level, flowers well above water level.
7. Floating, requiring no soil, grow outside in summer, must be wintered in warm house.

Aquatic plants   The classification is according to the depth of the pool, and the way in which the plants grow, in, under or over the water.

1. *Depth of water* 3-5 *in. Flowers and foliage above the water.*

Acorus calamus

Alisma plantago-aquatica

Anthemis

Brazenia (Flowers and foliage are floating)

Butomus

Calla

Caltha

Cyperus

Dracocephalum

Eriophorum

Glyceria

Hydrocotyle

Hypericum

Iris laevigata

I. pseudacorus

Juncus

Jussieua

Lysimachie

Mentha aquatica

Menyanthes

Mimulus luteus

Miscanthus

Myosotis

Nesaea

Orontium

Oxalis (Flowers and foliage are floating)

Peltrandra

Phragmites

Ranunculus aquatilis

Rorippa

Rumex

Sagittaria

Saururus

Scirpus

Typha

2. *Depth of water* 12-15 *in.*

Aponogeton (Flowers and foliage float).

Hippuris (Flowers and foliage are well above the surface).

Hydrocleis (Flowers and foliage float).

Limnanthemum (Flowers and foliage float).

Ranunculus lingua (Flowers and foliage are above the surface).

Sparganium (Flowers and foliage are above the water).

Villarsia (Flowers and foliage float).

3. *Submerged Aquatics.*

These are those plants whose flowers and foliage are borne under the surface of the water.

Apium

Callitriche

Ceratophyllum

Elodea

Ericaulon

Fontinalis

Litorella

Mayaca

Myriophyllum*

Najas

Oenanthe*

Potamogeton

Ranunculus

Sagittaria

Utricularia

* The flowers of these two plants are above water.

Submerged oxygenators The submerged oxygenating aquatic plants are most essential to every pool. They absorb the carbon dioxide and retain the carbon for their own growth, returning the oxygen to the water. Bubbles of pure oxygen can often be seen coming out from the leaves of such plants under the influence of sunlight. If they are kept healthy, such plants will work every day to keep the water clear, and make it unnecessary for the pool owner to empty and clean the pool as frequently as he would normally have to do.

Submerged aquatics provide the necessary shelter and shade for young fish and are suitable 'homes' for the deposition of the spawn. Fish are always cannibalistic, but the babies can dart amongst the submerged plants and so elude the older fish, until they are large enough to fight for themselves. Many of these submerged plants are also a necessary source of food for fish, and provide them with the mineral salts they require.

Three plants that fish are particularly fond of are the common watercress, the elodeas and the callitriche. Care should be taken never to introduce duckweed and azolla into a pool. Both spread too rapidly, and so will cover the surface of the pool with green leaves and rob it of its powers of reflection.

Lists of submerged oxygenating aquatics are now given. **A list of oxygenating aquatics for water gardens** They are marked according to whether they grow outside only, or in indoor aquaria. Some species do well in either case.

(*) Denotes OUTSIDE.   (†) Denotes INDOOR.

*	Apium nodiflorum	*	Oenanthe fistulosa
*†	A. inundatum	*†	Potamogeton crispus
*†	Callitriche aquatica	*	P. natans
*†	Ceratophyllum demersum	*†	Ranunculus aquatilis
*†	Elodea callitrichoides	*	Rorippa
*	E. crispa	*	Sagittaria natans
*†	Eriocaulon septangulare	*	S. subulata
*†	Hottonia palustris	*†	Utricularia vulgaris
*	Myriophyllum spicatum		

For detailed descriptions of these plants turn to pages 151-64.

Floating aquatics Some aquatics float on the surface of the water and will grow in the water either with or without soil. Most of them grow masses of attractive foliage, and so provide shade and food for the fish, and incidentally for any other inhabitants there may be in the pool. Some floating aquatics are not hardy and have to be taken into a warm greenhouse during the winter. Others, on the other hand, are perfectly hardy, and it is these that are listed below.

The flowers and foliage of this group are borne on or under the surface, but do not root into the soil.

> Azolla
> Hydrocharis morsus-ranae
> Riccia

Hardy orchids

Most people seem to have an idea that orchids are hothouse flowers, and that it is impossible to grow them in the garden. Actually, there are many hardy varieties which will grow quite well around the pool. Most of them like the moist situation and will grow well in a compost consisting of equal parts of good soil and rotted leaf-mould. In addition, the surface of the soil should be covered with living sphagnum moss. The following plants are perhaps the pick of the hardy available varieties:

> Cephalanthera rubra
> Cypripedium acaule (Ladies' Slipper)
> C. spectabile
> Habenaria psycodes (Hinged Orchis)
> Orchis foliosa

Insectivorous bog plants

These 'insect-eating' plants are most fascinating and may be planted around the edge of a pool in a compost consisting of peat and chopped sphagnum moss. Unfortunately most of them are half-hardy, and so have to be taken into the greenhouse for the winter. All are best planted in full sun.

> Dionaea muscipula (Venus' Fly Trap)
> Drosera rotundifolia (Sundew)

15 Fish and Pool Scavengers

No one would consider having a pool without its complement of hardy fish. Fishes do help also to ensure the correct balance of nature, and are most attractive when swimming about in clear water. It is possible to keep many different varieties of fish, all of which will live together in peace, and the beauties of the different fish are set off one by another. But it is a great mistake to attempt to have too many fish. The best way of estimating the correct number is to realize that it is only possible to have 1 in. of fish (that is leaving out the tail) to every gallon of water. It is much better to have fewer fish, and for them all to be healthy and fit, than to have large numbers of fish, many of which will die or will suffer badly.

As fish get older their body bulk – that is their width and depth – naturally increases disproportionately to their length, and so this rule of 1 in. of fish per gallon does not hold good. Always understock a pool so as to allow for increase in weight, and there is always the chance that youngsters will come along to increase the numbers. Healthy fish should always have the opportunity of swimming a length eight times their length, that is to say, if a fish is 3 in. long, the pool should be at least 24 in. long.

Fortunately, in the garden pool there is little trouble in this direction, and as the surface area of the pool is usually large, there is an increased oxygenating power which allows for the increase in the size of the fish, as a rule.

It has already been said that all kinds of fish can be introduced, but if it is intended to have different kinds, the fish when put into the water should all be of approximately the same size. Just like boys at school, the large ones have a tendency to bully the small ones. Such bullying usually leads to the smaller fish being starved.

It is always better to purchase fish for a pool that have already been living in a pool, rather than to get hold of fish that have been brought up in a large lake or in a running stream. Such fish may be diseased or may be covered with fish lice. Fishes taken from rivers and streams do not like garden pool conditions, where there is no water movement.

Feeding

When fish have been first introduced, the beginner always tends to overfeed. It is when the hobby loses its novelty that the fish are in danger of starving! The real danger of over-feeding is not that the fish get too fat, but that the uneaten food will go bad and so encourage the growth of fungi.

Fishes eat much less in the winter than in the summer, for in their natural habitat food is much scarcer at this time of the year. For the same reason, fish are more sluggish in the winter than in the summer. It is only necessary during the winter months to give a pinch of fish food on a sunny day, and if it is found that the food is eaten readily, then a little more can be given. In the summer they should be fed regularly just like any other domestic 'animal'. The wise pool owner will feed the fish at regular times of the day, a good time being in the early evening. Regular feeding times lead to tameness, and the fish will collect at the side of the pool at feeding time in a fascinating manner.

Do not be tempted just to throw food in one mass at one point. If you do, the fish will not get the exercise they ought to have in chasing after their meal. Be sure to scatter the food over as large an area as possible. This even distribution allows the smaller fish to 'get a look in'.

Scald all dried food, or allow it to soak thoroughly before use. It then swells before being eaten, and so prevents indigestion and constipation. This is not really necessary with the hardy types of fish, but is desirable where fancy breeds are kept. The Celestials, the Fantails and the Telescopes, for instance, have bodies with abnormal internal organs, and it is these fish that can easily become ill if fed with dried food. That is why I am not recommending these unusual types.

Some fish are carnivorous, and must have a diet of live food. Typical examples are the Dog Fish, Cat Fish, and various types of the Bass family. But once again I don't recommend buying them. Most other fish are omnivorous and so require animal food and vegetable food. This may be provided by some of the proprietary fish foods, which are easy to purchase. In addition to the proprietary brands, give a little powdered vermicelli, or a small handful of some cereal once a month or so.

It is always wise to stock the pool with water fleas and lice, because these are rich in protein and will keep the fishes supplied with food during holiday periods. In addition, small, red worms, maggots and fresh ant eggs may be given. The dried ant eggs so often sold are of little value, for the husks are soon passed back by the fish, and so provide media for fungus growth. It should only be necessary to give the living food, i.e. the blood worms and the daphnia, once every three weeks or so, and then only during the warmest nine months of the year.

Exotic and native fish suitable for the pool

A list of suitable fishes for the pool

While, for the most part, the names given are those of hardy species, i.e. those that are able to remain in the pool all the year, some half-hardy ones are mentioned. Half-hardy types (which have a striking appearance) need to spend the winter in an indoor aquarium with a minimum water temperature of 65 degrees F.

When buying Goldfish or any livestock for the pool, always go to a reputable breeder. (I shall be happy to recommend good firms.) The reason for this is that the breeder's stock will have been reared and acclimatized to the vagaries of the American climate, whereas if fishes are purchased from abroad they may have been reared in warm water and intensively fed, and thus they are less likely to survive in cold water.

Do not buy undersized fishes as they suffer more from changes of temperature than their bigger brothers. This is particularly true in Northern conditions.

See that the fish has a symmetrical body. Look for bright eyes, liveliness, well-spread fins, and make sure that there is no depression behind the gill plates. (This can be seen when looking at the fish from above.) There should also be no depression on the lower side of the body near the anus.

Goldfish

Comet—A graceful fish with a long body, fins and tail. It looks 'streamlined', especially as it is an active fish, always on the move.

Shubunkin—A goldfish with transparent scales, usually sprinkled and mottled with red, brown, yellow, white and black. All these colours may not be on the same individual but may be developed later. An attractive fish for the pool and aquarium.

Bitterling—This is a very small carp and is sometimes known as the 'Rainbow Fish' because of its lovely colours.

Golden Orfe—This is gradually becoming more popular than the Goldfish, on account of its hardiness in withstanding severe winters. It is a beautiful salmon-pink and of lively habit.

Golden Rudd—This fish has striking colouring, being dark copper gold above and silvery beneath, the fins and tail being bright scarlet. The older the fish, the more intense the colours.

Scavengers

The various plants grown in the pool may be subject to insect pests and diseases. It is necessary to keep these in check, and much can be done in this direction if the pool is stocked with sufficient scavengers. There may be a surplus of algae. The water snails will prevent trouble here, for they feed on them. The mussels actually extract from the water minute particles of animal and vegetable matter, and are sometimes called because of this, the 'housekeepers' of the pool.

It may only be necessary to have a few snails. One per 5 gallons is the maximum number that should be added.

Actually, if two or three dozen are bought even for quite a large pool, they will do, for they breed quite freely.

The disadvantage of the mussel is that it does like to live in mud at the bottom of the pool. The small pool should not be muddy! Mussels will move about in the mud, and if they cannot get sufficient food at one place they will travel to another, blundering through and up-rooting plants that come in their way.

There are two kinds of lice, the fresh water lice and the fish lice. The fish lice are harmful and attack the fishes, but the fresh water lice are good scavengers and they provide foodstuff for the fish also. Water fleas are useful because they feed on the single cell algae, which discolour the water. These are not fleas in the ordinary sense of the word, and so need not be feared, but they do move with a curious jumpy motion in the water and thus have been given this name. Never collect water fleas from a pond in the country in order to introduce them into your pool, for in so doing you may easily gather other living organisms that are harmful.

Two harmful pests one should fear particularly are (1) the fish louse (described later) and (2) the leech. Leeches often attach themselves to fish, particularly around the eyes. They swim with a ribbon-like movement and move along the edge of the pool by looping their bodies forward like a looper caterpillar. It is almost impossible to get rid of leeches once they are in the pool and the only thing to do is to empty the pool and start all over again.

As there are many water creatures that can be housed in the pool, and most of them are interesting, it is advisable to list and describe them individually.

List of pool scavengers

Fresh Water Louse (Asellus aquaticus)—A grand scavenger. Provides good food for the fish. This species is harmless to fish and must not be confused with the Fish Louse which attacks the fish themselves.

Fresh Water Shrimp (Gammarus pulex)—Resembles a sea-shrimp. A good scavenger and excellent fish food.

Fresh Water Whelk (Limnaea auricularia stagnalis)— A handsome type of snail which feeds on decaying animal matter. Scavenges well and breeds prolifically. There is some danger of the pond becoming over-populated with whelks, unless they can be controlled. They can damage lily leaves.

Fresh Water Winkle (Paludina vivipara)—Looks like a snail, with brown bands. The youngsters are born alive and are sometimes $\frac{1}{4}$ in. long when they appear. A useful scavenger. Can damage the lily leaves.

Ramshorn Snail (Planorbis corneus)—Probably the best scavenging snail, as it feeds entirely on decayed animal and vegetable matter.

Non-scavengers *Newt (Triton vulgaris)*—Feeds on all kinds of insect larvae and may also be given finely chopped meat and baby worms. A suitable inhabitant for the small pool. May well appear – or you may be able to 'find' your own in a nearby pond.

Water Fleas (Daphnia)—Tiny little creatures which dart about in a jumpy manner in the water. They are excellent live food for all aquatic animals.

Mayfly Larvae (Ephemeria vulgata)—This is excellent food for all kinds of fish and so should be encouraged in every pool. May be bought from aquatic specialists.

16 Buying a Complete 'Set' for your Pool

1 **A round pool** 6 ft. in diameter and 2 ft. deep in the middle.

PLANTS. One pink lily in the middle. Around it 4 portions of submerged oxygenating plants (examples – Elodea sp., Myriophyllum sp., Ceratophyllum demersum or Hottonia palustris).

FISH. Not more than 12 x 2in. - 3 in. fish.

2 **A rectangular pool** 10 ft. long and 4 ft. wide, 2½ ft. deep at one end, sloping to 1½ ft. at the other.

PLANTS. Two lilies – one pink, one white. 12 portions of submerged oxygenating plants (taken from the examples shown in 1 above). Marginal plants dependent upon the space available in the shallow end, but, as a guide, 8 plants (examples – Butomus umbellatus, Glyceria spectabilis var., Scirpus zebrinus, Sagittaria japonica, Iris, Calla palustris, Pontederia cordata, Typha minima, Mimulus sp.). 1 Floating plant such as Hydrocharis morsus-ranae or Stratiotes aloides.

FISH. Not more than 15 x 4 in. - 5 in. fish (or equivalent size).

3 **A large pool** 15 ft. by 8 ft., 3 ft. deep in the centre, sloping to 2 ft. at one end and 1 ft. at the other.

PLANTS. One lily for the middle – Red (e.g. Escarboucle); one lily for the 2 ft. end – Yellow (e.g. M. chromatella); one lily for the 1 ft. end – White (e.g. Candida). 20 portions of submerged oxygenating plants (taken from examples in 1 above plus Potamogeton crispus, Callitriche sp. and Ludwigia palustris as additional choices).

Plants for the 1 ft. end : 12 Plants from the selection in 1 and 2 above plus Lythrum salicaria, Saururus cernuus, Acorus calamus sp., Sagittaria japonica fl. pleno.

Plants for the 2 ft. end : Aponogeton distachyon or plants with surface floating leaves such as potamogeton natans, Sagittaria sagittifolia, Polygonum amphibium (other marginal plants normally for shallower areas as described above could be used if planted in baskets or on a shelf so that the depth of water was effectively reduced). 4 Floating plants such as Azolla sp., Stratiotes aloides or Hydrocharis morsus-ranae.

FISH. Not more than 24 fish of 5 in. - 6 in. long or equivalent.

4 **Tub** 30 in. across and 18 in. deep.

PLANTS. One Pigmy yellow lily (such as Pygmaea hel-vola) and 2/3 portions submerged oxygenating plants from selection in 1 above.

FISH. Not more than 4 x 2 in. - 3 in. fish.

I have not suggested species of fish as this is a matter of personal choice, but for the small pools 1 and 4 it is suggested that Goldfish or Shubunkins would prove most satisfactory. For 2 and 3 one might consider in addition Golden Orfe which are most attractive surface feeding fish but do like plenty of space. Golden Rudd are also worthy of consideration and, if a scavenger is required, Green Tench are very suitable.

In making these recommendations I have erred on the side of understocking rather than overstocking the pools since water plants, once well established, will spread and fish will grow. Also, in any event, more can be added later if necessary.

I have left out any reference to Mollusca. They should not be introduced into the pool until the plants are well established. The following quantities are more appropriate :—

Pool 1. – 12 Planorbis Corneus or Paludina Sp.

Pool 2. – 24 Planorbis Corneus or Paludina Sp.

Pool 3. – 36 Planorbis Corneus or Paludina Sp.

Pool 4. – I would not be inclined to have snails in this small tub otherwise the Pygmaea hel-vola might disappear rather rapidly.

17 Health in the Pool

You can usually tell when a fish is healthy, for it carries its fin erect and its tail fully expanded. But if you happen to see a fish swimming sluggishly or moping in some corner, then you may suspect trouble. The simplest way to settle the 'tummy troubles' of a fish is to give it a dose of Epsom salts. Some of these crystals should be thrown in at the regular feeding time instead of the food. The fish gobble them up, and within a day or so are usually quite well again. The fasting seems to do them no harm at all.

Enemies

Fishes have enemies which live on them and weaken them. The most common is the louse.

FISH LOUSE (Argulus foliacens). This parasite is about the size of a pin's head and up to $\frac{1}{4}$ in. long. Each louse is flattened, transparent and has four pairs of legs and two little, bold black eyes. The louse attaches itself to the fish and sucks and sucks and so debilitates its host. Once a fish is debilitated it is subject to attacks of other pests and diseases.

Control. There is no satisfactory method of control. Once lice have infested the pool, all that can be done is to empty out the whole pool and clean it *thoroughly*. It is a great mistake to introduce sticklebacks or any fish from wayside ponds, as this is the most common method of introducing fish lice.

FROGS. These may be a nuisance as they can scratch the fish, which will afterwards develop a fungus disease and die. Always keep frogs out at mating time by putting a $\frac{1}{2}$-in. nylon mesh over the pool. At mating time frogs clasp and scratch such fish as roach in pools. It is usually the male frogs that do this.. This $\frac{1}{2}$-in. netting all over the pool at mating time will keep them away.

LEECHES. There are many different kinds of leeches. Some are 3 in. long and others smaller. All are vicious. The smaller ones curl themselves up into an insignificant ball and so may be introduced into the pool unwittingly. The mouth is really a circular sucking disc, and the insect has horny teeth. The leeches can be seen swimming about with a wavy movement.

Control. Cut off any leeches seen on fish as close as possible and carefully clean out the pool. Start again with completely fresh water.

N.B.—Planaria, a creature rather like a leech, may be

found on the underside of a water lily leaf. It is not harmful and can be distinguished from the ordinary leech by
the fact that it is all in 'one piece' and not at all segmented.
In addition it has no sucking disc.

HYDRA. When feeding the inhabitants of a pool with
live insects, Hydra sometimes are introduced because they
can turn themselves into tiny circular 'bags'. They can
look like baby anemones or tiny octopi. They do very little
harm to the big fish, but they do consume baby fishes and
large numbers of water fleas.

Control. Clean out the pool completely. Refill with
clean water. Be very careful when carrying out live feeding.

Self-visiting enemies

Some pests are difficult to keep out of the pool. They
fly from other gardens, and though they may just pay a
passing call, they may become permanent unwanted visi-
tors. Take, for instance, the Water Beetle and the Water
Bug. Even if they only visit the pool for an hour or so,
they may lay their eggs, and then large numbers of 'maggots' hatch out. These maggots later turn into beetles
which go on living in the pool for years. They prey on the
pond life and can become a regular nuisance.

WATER BEETLE (Dytiscus marginalis). This feeds on
other insect life, as does its larva which is about 1½ in. long
and of a dirty yellow colour. The beetle is dark brown with
a little yellow edge, the underside of its body being lighter.
These beetles have been known to attack quite large fish.

Control. By using a small shrimping net, you can lie
down beside the pool on a sunny day, and when the beetles
come to the surface for air scoop them up and kill them.

WATER BUG (Noctonecta and Corixa). The former is
the Water Boatman, a fascinating creature whose rear
limbs, when in use, look like oars. Actually, it swims on
its back. The Corixa, on the other hand, though similar,
swims the right way up.

Control. As for Water Beetle.

DRAGON FLY. The larvae of the large dragon fly is
dirty grey and has six legs and a forked tail. The mouth
has a pair of false jaws which cover the face and so are
called by some people 'a mask'. The larva attacks the fish
by clasping it with its jaws.

Control. Try to prevent the dragon fly from visiting

the pond in daytime and always catch any larvae that can be seen.

Diseases

Unfortunately, there are several diseases to which fish are liable.

BLADDER TROUBLE. Fish with bladder trouble behave in a most extraordinary manner. They roll about in the water, sink to the bottom and rise to the top. They swim erratically and may shiver and shake.

Control. Give a stimulating bath as described on page 150. See that the water is so shallow that it only just covers the dorsal fin of the fish when stretched fully. Add to the bath 1 teaspoonful of Epsom salts per gallon of water, and try to keep the temperature round about 60 degrees F. As in the case of congestion, gradually increase the temperature of the water if necessary.

CONGESTION. The fish will become slow moving and the fins will be depressed. Blood blotches may be seen on the fins and about the body. The fish may lose colour and the gills may be inflamed. This disease is like pneumonia in human beings and is often caused through moving the fish from one pool to another one where the temperature is lower. Congestion can be brought about by sudden changes of temperature.

Control. Give the fish a stimulating bath as described on page 150. The temperature of the water should be about 55 degrees F. Should the outside water be well below this, successive baths should be given day by day, the temperature of the water being increased slightly each time.

CONSTIPATION. When the droppings of fish seem to hang from its anus and do not fall away naturally, then constipation may be feared.

Control. Start giving some live food immediately. In addition add $\frac{1}{2}$ oz. of Epsom salts per 5 gallons of water.

SHOCK. Many fish suffer from shock, especially if children worry them by poking about in the pool with sticks. If they are badly handled through trying to net them, they can also suffer from shock. Fish sometimes leap out of the water and lie on the surface as if dead, or they may extend their gills and make their fins taut and turn over. Such symptoms are seen after extraordinarily severe thundery weather.

Control. Put two to three drops of brandy or sal volatile

down the throat of the fish and place it in a stimulating bath.

TAIL AND FIN ROT. A bacterium infects the tail or fin and rotting takes place.

Control. When rotting is bad, place the stump on the edge of a table and cut the diseased parts of the fins away with a razor blade. Then paint the stump with Friars Balsam and keep the treated area above the water until it dries. In time the fin will grow again.

In mild cases, dip the affected parts into turpentine for ten seconds and then into hydrogen peroxide for ten seconds, or, instead, paint the affected parts with a camel hair brush. Wash away the two solutions with fresh warm water afterwards. Make certain that neither the peroxide nor the turpentine gets into the gills or eyes. If the fish can be held in a piece of wire netting with the head and the gills just below the surface of the water during treatment, it will not suffer as much as if it was taken right out of the water.

WHITE FUNGUS. A white fuzzy growth appears on the fins and spreads all over the body to the gills, where it proves fatal.

Control. Take affected fish out of the pool directly they show signs of infection and put them in a basin of fresh water, adding 1 oz. of table salt to every gallon. Let the fish remain there until they show signs of distress and then remove them and place in fresh water. All other fish that have been in contact with infection, should be placed in a bowl of water coloured deep pink with permanganate of potash. Again these are left there until they show signs of distress and they may then be kept in quarantine for a week or two in clean water to see if they show signs of disease or not.

Experts use Phenoxethol at the rate of 1 cu. cm. to 99 cu. cm. of distilled water. From this solution use 10 cu. cm. per quart of aquarium water. When changing water, it is always necessary to be certain that the temperature is exactly the same. In the winter the treatment may be given with water of a higher temperature, but this ought to be done gradually. Then when the fish is cured, the water should be changed gradually again to colder water before the fish is put back in the pool. It is always wise to use a net when removing fish from one bath to another, for catching fish in one's hand can do more harm than the disease.

After the fish has convalesced, it may be rather weak, thus a stimulating bath should be given. Eight drops of sweet spirit of nitre and eight drops of ammonia should be placed in the bowl per gallon of water. This invigorating bath should last twenty-four hours. In ordinary cases, one bath of this kind is sufficient, but where fish are very, very weak, three may be necessary. Such treatment gives increased appetite, helps respiration and accelerates the blood circulation.

WHITE SPOT. This is really a parasite which enters the outer skin of a fish and feeds on the blood. A colony is thus raised and it is then that the tiny white spots will be seen on the fins and the body of the fish.

Control. This is a much easier disease to control in the aquarium than in the pool. Fish should be removed from a pool and put in a temporary bowl so that the parasites can be starved – this should happen within a week. Affected fish may be isolated, and after two days may be removed and laid very carefully on a soft cloth, and the affected parts should then be painted with a strong solution of bicarbonate of soda. This should then be washed off with clean water at a temperature of 60 degrees F., but this must be poured away from the gills and not towards them. The fish should now be returned to a bowl of clean water into which 8 drops of ammonia have been placed per gallon. This painting should be carried out once a day for four days and the cure should then be complete.

General Remarks. Fungus diseases may begin through careless handling and bruising through the attacks of other creatures in the pool, and through improper living conditions. The spores may be there the whole time, but they can only attack weakly or wounded fish.

There are large numbers of plants which may be used around and about a pool, many of which are very beautiful indeed. I have tried in this chapter to choose those that are (a) not too expensive and (b) easy to grow.

ACORUS. A hardy herbaceous, water-loving plant. Best grown in shallow water or moist loamy soil.

A. Calamus (Sweet Flag or Bee Wort). Height 2-3 ft. Broad straplike leaves. Greenish flowers. Aromatic.

A. Calamus var. variegatus. Grassy foliage is cream and yellow. Less aromatic.

A. gramineus. Dwarfer and slenderer variety, 8 to 12 in. in height. Grown in very shallow water or at the water edge.

ALSIMA (Water Plantain). Whorls of pinky white flowers and plantain-like leaves. Height 2-3 ft.. Grows by margins of rivers, lakes and ponds. As they reproduce themselves very easily by seed, the dead flower heads should be removed. Flowers in summer.

A. lanceolatum. 12-18 in. Slender spear-like leaves and pinky white flowers.

A. plantago-aquatica. Large stalked leaves. Spikes of delicate rose coloured flowers. 2-3 ft. Flowers in summer.

ANACHARIS. See Elodea.

ANTHEMIS (Chamomile). Hardy annual. Upright habit. Narrow leaves and small flowers in June.

A. cotula. Tufts of lanceolate leaves. Small double yellow flowers. Annual but seeds itself yearly. Wet soil or shallow water. 10 in.

A.c. coronopifolia. Annual, seeds itself yearly. Small yellow flowers. Wet soil or shallow water. 6-10 in. approx.

APIUM (Marshwort). The foliage is submerged and the flowers are just above the surface. The leaves are finely dissected and spread out fanlike in the water. Plant in shallow water.

A. inundatum (lesser Apium). For winter and spring planting. Later in the year, the slender stem and leaves appear above the surface. The white flowers are borne above the surface.

APONOGETON. Spikes of sweet scented flowers emerging among flat, floating leaves. Flowers in April and October.

A. distachyon. Large racemes of white, V-shaped flowers with black anthers. Oval leaves. Scent like May blossom.

ASTILBE. A member of the Saxifrage family. Useful bog and waterside plant, similar in appearance to Spiraea. Flowers are crimson, pink, or white, in summer.

A. Arendsii. Includes named varieties.

Bremen. Salmon red. 2½ ft.

Granat. Dark crimson. 3½ ft.

King Albert. White. 6-7 ft.

A. chinensis pumila. Erect flower-spikes, lilac rose. Dwarf habit. 1 ft.

AZOLLA (Fairy Moss). Floats on the surface like a moss-green carpet. Before dying down in the autumn, the foliage goes red brown. Reproduces itself yearly. It is not recommended for small ponds, as it spreads so rapidly as to become a possible nuisance. Is best bought and planted in June-July.

A. caroliniana. Fronds are ½ to 1 in. in length, of a lacy texture. They are first, pale green and later red.

BRAZENIA. An interesting species, but difficult to establish.

B. Schreberi. Small, oval floating leaves. Flowers are about ½ in. across, purple. Will grow in 4-6 ft. of water.

BUTOMUS (Flowering Rush).

B. Umbellatus. Grows in 2-6 in. of water, and is 2-4 ft. tall. Handsome clusters of rose-pink flowers. Sword-like leaves, which are purple bronze when young and then turning green.

CALLA. (Bog Arum).

C. palustris. 9 in. in height and prefers shallow water or the water edge. Heart-shaped leaves. May not flower the first year, but the small arum-like flowers are followed by clusters of red berries.

CALLITRICHE (Starwort). Vivid green foliage, very dainty and star-tipped.

Callitriche Sp. Profusion of dainty fresh green foliage. Good outside oxygenator.

C. aquatica. Good oxygenator for indoor aquaria as well as for ponds etc.

CALOPOGON. A bog orchid needing a moist and shady

position. Should be disturbed as little as possible. Height 12-18 in.

    C. pulchellus. Crimson purple flowers with yellow, orange and purple hairs on lip. Flowers June-July.

CALTHA (Marsh Marigold). Flowers early.

    C. palustris. Common Marsh Marigold. 9-15 in. Flowers resemble large buttercups. Grows in wet soil by water.

    C.p. plena. Very free flowering. Yellow double flowers.

    C. polypetala. 2-3 ft. Dark green leaves 10-12 in. across. Large, golden flowers 3 in. across. Spreads very easily.

CAREX (Sedge Grass). 15 in. in height. Grass-like perennials to grow at the water edge or in wet soil.

    C. riparis Bowles' Golden. 15 in. Rich golden yellow foliage.

    C. paludosa. A shorter species. Bluish-green leaves and brownish black flower spikes. Hardy and decorative.

CEPHALANTHERA (Helleborine). Bog orchid bearing purple and white flowers in May.

CERATOPHYLLUM (Hornwort). Bristle-like leaves which are submerged. Will grow in very deep water. Requires careful handling, as is rather brittle.

    C. demersum. Small species but may grow to 1-2 ft., according to conditions. The flowers are inconspicuous but the fruit is horned, hence the name.

CYPERUS (Umbrella Grass). A sedge-like plant. Likes shallow water.

    C. longus. Tufts of grass-like foliage ending in plumes of reddish brown.

    C. vegetus. Broad, grass-like foliage, mahogany coloured plumes. Hardy and in character throughout the winter.

CYPRIPEDIUM. Some members of this orchidaceous group are suitable for water gardening. They like a very moist soil with peat, or chopped sphagnum moss incorporated, or leaf-mould.

    C. spectabile (Moccasin Orchid). A very hardy and beautiful orchid. Each stem bears 1-3 flowers of bright rose or crimson. Prefers shade, and is 15-24 in. in height.

DIONAEA MUSCIPULA (Venus' Fly Trap). Insectivorous plant. Flowerless, but has two lobes which are teethed. When an insect settles on a lobe, it is soon caught between the teeth and digested by the plant. Later the lobes re-open to release the remains of the victim. The plant is not hardy and should be grown in full sun on wet soil which has peat, leaf-mould, or chopped sphagnum moss in it.

DODECATHEON (American Cowslip). A member of the Primula family, it likes waterside or boggy situations. Spring flowering. Has rosettes of narrow leaves, and cyclamen-like flowers.

> *D. meadia.* 18 in. in height. Clusters of drooping, magenta flowers with reflexed petals. Long, green leaves freely spotted with purple.

DRACOCEPHALUM PALUSTRE (Dragon's Head). Light green foliage, spikes of rose pink flowers in the summer. Plant in shallow water. 1 ft. in height.

DROSERA ROTUNDIFOLIA (Sundew). Insectivorous. Traps its victims by means of a sticky fluid on its reddish leaves. Has delicate white flower.

EICHHORNEA CRASSIPES (Floating Water Hyacinth). Stout stems running over the surface. Spikes of lavender blue flowers. Not hardy and should be wintered in a greenhouse. Each flower has a 'peacock eye'.

ELODEA. Dark green, spiky foliage is submerged and remains in character through the winter. The plant, an excellent oxygenator, is apt to grow rather tall, so any dead or yellow foliage should be regularly removed. Is a submerged aquatic.

> *E. canadensis.* Serrated, oval leaves, light green when young and darker with age.
>
> *E. callitrichoides.* Pea green foliage. Excellent oxygenator.
>
> *E. crispa.* Narrow, reflexed leaves.

EPIPACTIS. This orchidaceous species should be grown in a sunny or partly shaded position in loam and humus in some form.

ERIOCAULON SEPTANGULARE (Pipewort). Oxygenator for outside and indoor aquaria. Pure white flowers, clusters of leaves, creeping rootstock.

ERIOPHORUM (Cotton Grass). Low growing plant with erect stems topped by snow white tufts. 12 in. Grows in shallow water.

> *E. angustifolium.* The most handsome of the group.

FONTINALIS (Willow Moss). A very attractive form of

Moss. Is a submerged aquatic and prefers some shade. Thrives best in running water.

> *F. antipyretica.* Greyish green with very long branched stems. Very leafy and the flowers are inconspicuous. Very ornamental, and provides good cover for small aquatic life.

GLYCERIA (Manna Grass). Perennial waterside plant. They flourish, so need to be kept under control.

> *G. aquatica var. variegata.* Very pretty, 18-24 in. tall. The foliage is regularly striped with green, yellow, and white, and suffused with a rose tint in the autumn. Roots need to be kept in control by occasional thinning.

HIPPURIS VULGARIS (Mare's Tail). Whorled stems with short, narrow leaves 6-9 in. in height. Grows in running water. Unusual plant.

HOTTONIA PALUSTRIS (Water Violet). Oxygenator for outside pools and indoor aquaria. Rosettes of pea green submerged, fern-like foliage. Height above water 6-12 in. White and lavender flowers. Grows in 4-18 in. of water.

HYDROCHARIS MORSUS-RANAE (Frogbit). A floating aquatic. Small, kidney-shaped leaves, bright green, $1\frac{1}{2}$ in. across. Small, three petalled white flowers. Very attractive, but snails are fond of eating the soft, spongy leaves.

HYDROCLEIS (Water Poppy).

> *H. commersoni.* Foliage floats on the surface. The leaves are dark green and heart shaped. Pale yellow, poppy-like flowers are well above the surface. Plant in 12-15 in. of water, and in a warm spot.

HYDROCOTYLE (Marsh Pennywort).

> *H. vulgaris.* Masses of foliage about 4 in. above water level and whorls or pretty, white flowers. Needs to be controlled. Grow in 2-4 in. of water or mud.

HYPERICUM (Marsh Hypericum).

> *H. elodes.* Close tufts of woolly foliage covered with white hairs. The terminals are of soft yellow flowers. Height 6 in. Grown in 2-4 in. of water or mud.

IRIS

> *I. laevigata.* Plant in wet soil or 3-4 in. of water. Height 2 ft. Rich blue flowers with golden spot on the claw. Thin and grassy foliage.

> *I.l. Snowdrift.* Large snow white blooms. Height about 2 ft.

I.l. albo purpurea. The rich blue of this variety is mottled with white.

I. versicolor. Rich claret/blue. Height about 1½ ft.

I.v. kermesina. Rich purple. Height about 2 ft.

I. sibirica sp. (Blue). Vivid blue flowers, carried on gracefully erect, slender stems. Grows best in damp soil only.

I.s. Snow Queen. Similar to Blue Iris Sibirica with white flowers.

I. pseudacorus. (The original Fleur-de-Lys of France). Grow in shallow water or pond edge. Height 2-3 ft. Fine in large clumps. Bright yellow flowers and sword-like leaves. May-June.

I. sibirica. Small, blue flowers. Green arching and tufted foliage. Very good for cut flowers. May-June.

I. sibirica var. Caesar. Violet purple flowers. Height 3 ft.

JUNCUS (Rushes). Generally nuisances and difficult to eradicate, but the species mentioned are unusual in appearance.

J. effusis var. spiralis. 18 in. stems twisted in a curious corkscrew manner. Grow in 3 in. of water.

JUSSIEUA (Water Evening Primrose). Grows in 3-5 in. of water. Flowers and foliage are above water. Most members are not hardy, but the one species given here is. Will grow in bog.

J. repens. Creeping masses of dark green foliage, spreading over surface, freely studded with gold yellow flowers. Needs to be controlled.

LEMNA (Duckweed). Ornamental and useful to aquatic life. No stems or leaves. Floats on surface. Multiplies rapidly and so should only be grown in large pools.

L. gibba. Thick Duckweed.

L. minor. Lesser Duckweed.

L. triscula. Ivy-leaved Duckweed and the best species. Good substitute for Riccia.

LIMNANTHEMUM. Member of the Gentian family. Has floating leaves and a profusion of small flowers. The roots should be confined or thinned occasionally.

L. nymphoides. 6-18 in. of water. Heart-shaped foliage, mottled and flat on the surface. The leaves are 2 in. across. The golden yellow flowers stand 2-3 in. above the water.

LOBELIA DORTMANNA. Grows in shallow water. Is a submerged oxygenating aquatic. Is 1 to 2 in. in height and has upright foliage, similar to the Litorella. Pale blue flowers, thin and wiry stems.

LUDWIGIA. Is a bog plant, but will grow under water. Very decorative foliage. Oval leaves in pairs, undersides are red, topsides green.

LYCOPUS (Gipsywort).

> *L. europus.* 9-12 in. tall. Deeply cut, lanceolate leaves. Whorls of pale lilac flowers.

LYSIMACHIA.

> *L. nummularia* (Creeping Jenny). A good carpeting plant for the waterside. Small rounded leaves in opposite pairs, which are ½-1 in. long. Bright gold cup-shaped flowers in the summer.

> *L. vulgaris* (Orange Loosestrife). 2 ft. tall. Handsome bog plant and good for pond margins. Large heads of cup-shaped flowers (yellow).

LYTHRUM (Loosestrife). They are ideal for masses in bogs or wild gardens.

> *L. salicaria* (Black Blood or Purple Loosestrife). Very showy with reddish purple blooms.

MAYACA. Prostrate aquatic. The crown is covered with 3-5 in. of water. The foliage is submerged but the flowers are above the surface. Not very hardy.

> *M. sellowina.* 6-9 in. Light green mossy foliage spangled with rosy flowers.

MENTHA (Mint). Generally grown as garden plants, but one or two species are suitable for the water garden.

> *M. aquatica* (Water mint). 1-4 ft. tall. Egg-shaped, serrated leaves and whorl of lilac flowers. This hairy species is strongly scented.

MENYANTHES (Bog Bean).

> *M. trifoliata.* Likes shallow water. Smooth, olive green foliage and leaves borne in trefoils. Flowers are in clusters and are pure white within and pink on the outside. The stamens are red. The plant is of striking appearance.

MIMULUS (Water Musk). A water-loving plant which grows in wet soil or shallow water.

> *M. cardinalis.* Has hoary foliage and clusters of red and yellow flowers. 18 in. Tall and very showy.

> *M. ringens.* Flowers of delicate lavender blue carried gracefully on tall erect stems.

> *M. luteus.* Taller than the above and carries yellow

flowers frequently spotted with red. 9-12 in.

MISCANTHUS (Eulalia). Tall grasses allied to Sugar Cane. Are at their best if planted singly in a moist, sunny position and in very rich, deep compost. The crowns of the variegated species should be protected with leaves in the winter.

MYOSOTIS (Forget-me-not).

> *M. palustris.* Grows in shallow water. Light green foliage and clear blue flowers with yellow eyes.

MYRIOPHYLLUM (Milfoil).

> *M. proserpinacoides* (Parrot's Feather). Not hardy enough to survive a severe winter, although it is of rampant growth. Cuttings should be taken yearly in July from the growing tip and kept in a frostproof house for the winter. The leaves are a delicate whitish green and very feathery. In the late summer, the tips of the leaves turn crimson. They must be grown in a moist place and are favourite plants for raised pools or a fountain basin.

> *M. spicatum* (Water Milfoil). Green bronze foliage, rather tangled appearance. Flowers are pale green to white on thin spikes growing 3 in. out of water. When dormant, the buds are a clear red. A good oxygenator for ponds, etc.

NESAEA (Decodon). (Swamp Loosestrife, Water Willow.)

> *N. verticillata.* Handsome shrubby perennial. It has long wands which gracefully bend over and take root from the tip. Lanceolate in the axils. In the autumn, the foliage turns brilliant crimson.

NYMPHAEA (Water Lily). See separate list of Water-Lilies (pages 130-3).

OENANTHE. Fairly good oxygenator. Has attractive foliage.

> *O. fistulosa* (Water Dropwort). Pretty, green carrot-like foliage and a submerged aquatic.

ORCHIS. Requires rich leafy soil, moist but not wet, and partial shade, unless otherwise indicated.

> *O. foliosa.* Dark green foliage. Stems 2-3 ft. long with spikes of rose purple flowers, spotted white in May. Full sun when planting out.

ORONTIUM (Golden Club). This will grow in 12-18 in. of water or at pond edge. The roots go down very deep, therefore a good subsoil is essential. Once established, they are very difficult to lift again.

> *O. aquaticum.* Grows at pond edge. 12-18 in. tall, but in deep water the leaves sometimes float flat on the surface. The foliage is dark, velvety green, with silvery undersides, and so coated with wax that it is impervious to water. The flowers are early and are yellow.

OXALIS. The leaves have an acid taste.

> *O. natans.* Grown in 3-6 in. of water. Dwarf. The foliage is glaucous and clover-like. The flowers are small and white, and they float on the surface.

PELTANDRA (Arrow Arum). A sub-aquatic for shallow water at the pond edge. Glossy foliage. Should be grown in clumps. The flowers are like arums and have similar berries in the autumn. The flowers are known as spathes.

> *P. virginica* (Green Arrow Arum). Bright green, narrow leaves 4 in. long by 3 in. to 8 in. wide. Thick fibrous roots. Green spathes, long and tapering, never opening properly, and succeeded by green berries. Height 2½ ft. Best in swamps or shallow water.

PHRAGMITES (Reed). Has a hedge-like growth.

> *P. communis* (Common Reed). 6-10 ft. tall and makes good 'game' cover. Broad glossy leaves and heavy, purple or violet plumes of flowers. Often used on sandy shores on account of its 'binding' quality.

POA AQUATICA (Reed Poa). Ornamental grass-like reed for shallow water and moist places in the wild garden. The flower stems are very useful for indoor decoration.

POLYGONUM (Willow Grass). When this is planted in 1-2 ft. of water, the flowers and foliage float on the surface, but in shallower water the sprays are above the surface.

> *P. amphibium.* A popular species. Dark green foliage, oblong, turning purplish red. The rose-coloured flowers are on spikes.

PONTEDERIA (Pickerel Plant). Very decorative.

> *P. cordata.* The best blue-flowered aquatic. It does not become untidy nor is it rampant in growth. Height 18-24 in. The arum-like leaves are smooth, shining, and olive green in colour. It should be planted in mud under 3-5 in. of water at the pond edge.

POTAMOGETON (Pondweed). A submerged aquatic. Most of the species are very weedy and of such rapid growth as to destroy choicer plants, but some others are fairly suitable for ponds and aquaria as oxygenators. Most of them seem to prefer a clay subsoil, and are brittle to handle. The foliage is attractive in appearance.

P. *crispus* (Curled Pondweed). The common Pondweed. It has wavy edged, clear leaves, 3-4 in. long and ½ in. wide. These are massed on branching stems. The leaves are green, or, in a strong light, reddish-brown. This plant is specially useful to give colour in the winter. It can also be used for indoor aquaria.

P. *natans* (Broad Pondweed). Has attractive, floating leaves, either green or coppery red. Suitable for ponds and aquaria, but should not be introduced if it cannot be controlled, otherwise it may be rampant in growth.

PRIMULA (Primrose). The members of this family are very popular as waterside plants and provide colour in the spring. As they are of varying heights, it is best to plant groups of the taller sorts to separate the smaller varieties. Primulas require a rich, cool soil that is moist without being sodden. Therefore good drainage is needed and this will also prevent the sourness of soil that these plants dislike. Most prefer partial shade or woodlands.

P. *aurantica*. A dwarf Chinese species, 9 in. tall. It has reddish stems, dark green leaves, and orange-red flowers in the spring. It likes partial shade.

P. *beesiana*. This also is a Chinese bog primula, and produces whorls of fragrant, carmine flowers in May-June. Height 2 ft.

P. *bulleyana*. This likes to grow near water. It has thin, papery leaves, and buff-orange flowers in June. Height 18-24 in.

P. *denticulata* (Himalayan Primrose). Coarse foliage from which emerge stems bearing globular clusters of lilac flowers in April-May. Height 1-2 ft.

P. *japonica*. This is perhaps the most popular of the bog primulas.. Its appearance is very showy, and it is very hardy. The best position for this plant is massed along a waterside bank which is cool and moist and partially shaded. Tier after tier of crimson, pink, or white flowers are thrown up through May-June. There are named varieties for the colours. Height 2-3 ft.

P. *pulverulata*. Is similar to the above, but has mealy

stems carrying rich crimson flowers. 'Bartlett's Strain', a varietal group, gives other colours, i.e. apricot buff, rose pink, and salmon. There is a long flowering season in May. This species is suitable for the lower part of rockeries as well as along the banks of streams. Height 3½ ft.

P.p. Red Hugh. A charming variation of the type. Bright crimson flowers in May-June. Height 2 ft.

P. sikkimensis (Himalayan Cowslip). One of the most beautiful primulas. It likes wet boggy ground and has rosettes of long, narrow leaves, slender stems bearing clusters of fragrant, nodding flowers of pale yellow, each bloom being 1 in. in length and ½ in. across. These are out in June. Height 18-24 in.

RANUNCULUS. There are different species for different growing conditions and the varieties will be given under the appropriate heading. The name is said to originate from the fact that these plants grow in places favoured by frogs.

(a) SUBMERGED AQUATICS

R. aquatilis. A good oxygenator. The foliage is of two types : the submerged leaves are divided into hair-like segments, whilst the upper leaves are three-leaved and floating. These flowers are small, floating and white with yellow stamens. This plant grows in shallow bogs as well as running water, and is at its best from the autumn to the spring. Very hardy.

(b) GROWN IN OR NEAR WATER

R. lingua (Great Spearwort). A fine bold plant with large buttercup-like leaves. For large ponds only. Medium to tall in height.

R. flammula. Similar to *R. lingua,* but smaller, usually less than 1 ft. in height.

(c) HARDY SPECIES FOR WATERSIDE OR BOG GARDEN

R. aconitifolius var. flore pleno (Fair Maids of France and Kent). Double white flowers. Dark green leaves rather palm-like. Likes a moist spot by the waterside.

RICCIA. A floating aquatic. Not very hardy.

R. fluitans. Has masses of pale green foliage, no flowers, and is rather moss-like in appearance.

RUMEX (Dock). This plant is not specially useful but sometimes is planted for bold effects along the waterside.

R. hydrolapathum (Great Water Dock). 4-6 ft. tall. It has dark green, dock-like leaves which turn red in the autumn. The very large flower heads should be removed to prevent seeding.

SAGITTARIA (Arrowhead). The name refers to the arrow-shaped leaves. Most of the plants in this group grow in 5-6 in. of water. A few are very good oxygenators, particularly in the indoor aquaria.

(a) GOOD OXYGENATORS

S. natans. This is a very good oxygenator and is active for the greater part of the year. It has slender, grass-like leaves only a few inches tall. The flowers are in a single whorl and are white. It is not hardy but is good in the indoor aquarium.

S. subulata. This plant is popular on account of its diminutive height, and dark green foliage which is grassy in appearance. The stronger the light, the less height it attains. Provides good cover for small fry.

(b) FOR GROWING IN SHALLOW WATER

S. japonica (Japanese Arrowhead). Erect, glossy leaves, arrow-shaped, with a conspicuous spike of white flowers with yellow centres, in the summer. It will grow in aquaria, bog garden or along the margins of lakes and pools. Height 2½ ft.

S.j. flore pleno. This beautiful form has much larger flowers than the last. Snow-white and fully double.

S. sagittifolia (Common Arrowhead). 18 in. tall. Long, arrow-shaped leaves, spikes of purple-centred flowers of white. The flowering season is from June onwards. It should be planted in a sunny position and makes a good marginal plant.

SAURURUS (Lizard's Tail). A pretty, hardy aquatic to grow in 2-4 in. of water.

S. cernuus (American Swamp Lily). 12-24 in. in height. Dense spikes of nodding, fragrant, white flowers in the summer. Bright heart-shaped foliage.

SCIRPUS (Bullrush). In the wild state, the Bullrush grows in marshes and on wet moors and bogs. The roots need restriction in the water garden.

S. lacustris. Has fat, dark green rushes. Height 3-8 ft. Umbels or chocolate brown flowers near the tops of the stems.

S. Tabernaemontanii var. zebrinus (Zebra Rush). A

Japanese species with stems alternately green and white. Height 4-5 ft. Looks most effective when massed in shallow water.

SEDUM VILLOSUM. One of the few members of this group to grow in a bog garden. Is 3-4 in. tall. Has small, green leaves and terminals of white and rose flowers.

SENECIO CLIVORUM. 3 ft. tall. A Chinese plant with large, shining leaves which are often 20 in. across. Stout stems carrying crowded heads of rich orange flowers. These bloom at intervals between July and September. Should be grown at the waterside.

SPARGANIUM (Bur-reed). Has sword-like leaves. Will grow in 12-15 in. of water with the foliage and flowers well above the surface. This plant is not specially attractive but is good in a wild garden or as 'cover' for game.

> *S. angustifolium.* Stout, branching stems. 3-8 ft. tall. Flat, grassy leaves.
>
> *S. ramosum* (Bede Sedge). Looks similar to Iris pseudocorus. Has erect, waving leaves, spiky heads of flowers and prickly fruit.

SPIRAEA ulmaria (Meadow-Sweet). Grows above the water line, not in water. An attractive subject for the marginal surrounds. Its profusion of creamy-white blooms have a strong fragrance. They all grow medium to tall in height.

STRATIOTES ALOIDES (Water Soldier). This is a very unusual plant. It has long, tapering serrated leaves, and flowers. It will grow either floating on the surface or attached to the bottom of the pond, or aquarium. If the plant has plenty of room to spread, it may exceed 12 in. diameter. The flowers are floating just under the surface of the water, looking like cacti dahlias. The colours of the flowers vary with age and environment. These plants should never be planted – they should merely be dropped into the water and they will find their own roothold.

TYPHA (Reedmace). Aquatic plants with creeping rootstock and long, poker-like heads. They make a stately picture if grown in colonies. To stop Typhas from overrunning the pool, they should be planted in large boxes or in specially prepared 'pockets'. They will grow best under 1-6 in. of water.

> *T. angustifolia.* 5-10 in. tall. A very graceful plant with slender linear leaves. The flower spikes are dark brown and monoecious (has male flowers and female flowers).

In this plant, the male and the female flowers are separated by several inches of stem.

T. latifolia (Cat o'Nine Tails). Often confused with Bullrush. The 'pokers' are very attractive and do not scatter seed until the following spring, when goldfinches may be seen clinging to the ripe heads. This species is most suitable for naturalizing in large stretches of water. Height 4-8 ft. The grassy leaves are 18-24 in. long and 1-1½ in. wide. The flowers are close, cylindrical spikes 6-9 in. in length and about 1 in. in diameter. The female flowers (light brown) are immediately above the male flowers (chocolate brown).

leaves and small, rusty brown flower spikes.

T. minima. 12-18 in. tall and so very useful in small pools in the shallows. The plant has narrow, rush-like

UTRICULARIA VULGARIS (Bladderwort). An insectivorous plant and a floating aquatic. It has bladders which trap water-fleas, etc, and extracts their juice to assist its own growth. It is a handsome plant with thin, hair-like leaves and a few tiny, yellow flowers above the surface of the water. It can be used as an oxygenating agent in both aquaria and ponds, etc.

VALLISNERIA. It has long tape-like leaves. A submerged aquatic, easily grown. The method of fertilization is unusual, as the male and female flowers are borne on separate plants. The latter are carried on the end of long, spiral stalks which rise to the surface ready for pollination. When the female flowers are above the water, the male flowers break off and also rise to the surface and pollination takes place. Then the spiral stems contract and the seeds are ripened under water. The plant is also a good oxygenator. It grows fairly well in sand at the bottom of the pond or aquaria but does better if there is loam under the sand.

V. spiralis. Grows in aquaria or in ponds in a sheltered spot. Light green ribbon-like foliage.

VERONICA BECCABUNGA (Brooklime). A succulent plant, 9-12 in. tall. It has oval glossy leaves and vivid blue flowers, and makes a good marginal or bog plant.

VILLARSIA NYMPHAEOIDES. A rare species with small, floating, lily-like leaves and yellow flowers. Will grow indoors or outside.

Index